The

Shakespeare

BIRTHDAY BOOK.

Methinks their is much reason in his sayings
Julius Cæsar, Act 3.

LONDON:
E. NISTER, 26 & 28, St Bride Street E.C.
AND ALL BOOKSELLERS.

PRYOR PUBLICATIONS
Specialist in Facsimile Reproductions

75 Dargate Road, Yorkletts, Whitstable,
Kent CT5 3AE, England
Tel. & Fax (01227) 274655
E-mail: alan@pryor-publications.co.uk
www.pryor-publications.co.uk
From the USA Toll Free Phone/Fax
1866 363 9007
Published by Pryor Publications
For © Heritage Books
www.heritagebooks.net
Tel 01285 642288

ISBN 1-905253-03-6

Kent Exporter of the Year Awards Winner
Shortlisted
International Business Awards
A full list of publications sent free on request.

The grace of heaven,
Before, behind thee, and on every hand,
Enwheel thee round!

Othello, Act 2, Sc. 1

January 1.

THERE is a tide in the affairs of men
  Which, taken at the flood, leads on to fortune.
  Julius Cæsar.

2.

LIKE as the waves make towards the pebbled shore,
So do our minutes hasten to their end.
  Sonnet.

3.

WORDS are easy, like the wind
  Faithful friends are hard to find.   *Sonnet*

4.

HE is as full of valour as of kindness.
  King Henry V.

5.

HE was my friend, faithful and just to me.
  Julius Cæsar.

6.

LOVE all, trust a few,
  Do wrong to none.
All's Well that Ends Well.

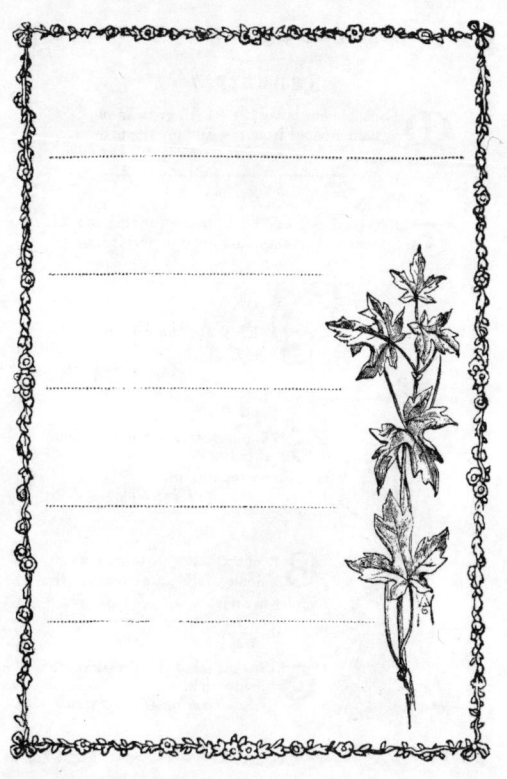

January 7.

MINE honour is my life; both grow in one;
Take honour from me, and my life is done.
King Richard II.

8.

TONGUES in trees, books in the running brooks,
Sermons in stones, and good in everything.
As You Like It.

9.

SWEET are the uses of adversity.
As You Like It.

10.

THE purest treasure mortal time afford
Is spotless reputation.
King Richard II.

11.

BE cheerful; wipe thine eyes:
Some falls are means the happier to arise.
Sonnet.

12.

TIS the mind that makes the body rich.
Taming of the Shrew.

January 13.

WHERE'ER I wander, boast of this I can—
  Though banished, yet a true-born Englishman.
  King Richard II.

14.

THE quality of mercy is not strained,
  It droppeth as the gentle rain from heaven
Upon the place beneath.

Merchant of Venice.

15.

LOVE thyself last.

King Henry VIII.

16.

NO legacy is so rich as honesty.
All's Well that Ends Well.

17.

STRIVING to better, oft we mar what's well.
King Lear.

18

THERE'S a divinity that shapes our ends,
Rough-hew them how we will.
Hamlet.

January 19.

THEY are but beggars that can count their worth;
But my true love is grown to such excess,
I cannot sum up half my sum of wealth.
Romeo and Juliet.

20.

THE sweetest lady that ever I looked on.

Much Ado About Nothing.

21.

BEAUTY is but a vain and doubtful good,
A shining gloss that vadeth suddenly.
Passionate Pilgrim.

22.

IF thou dost love, pronounce it faithfully.
Romeo and Juliet.

23.

WHAT stature is she of? Just as high as my heart. *As you Like It.*

24.

HE hath an excellent good name.

Much Ado about Nothing.

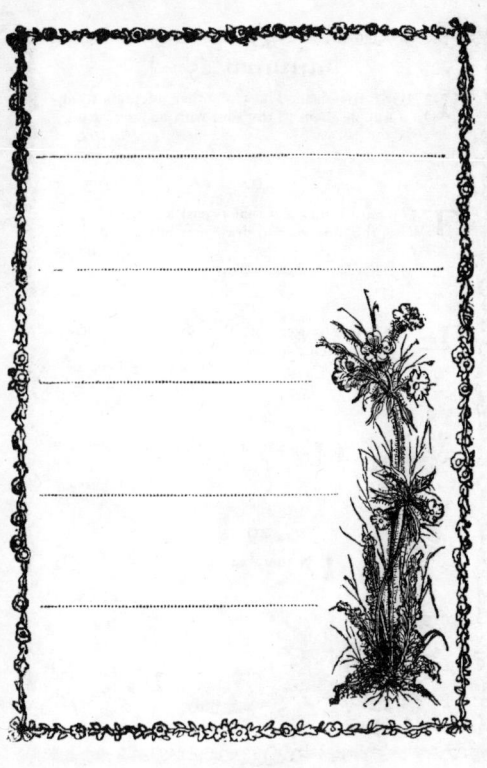

January 25

THOSE friends thou hast, and their adoption tried,
Grapple them to thy soul with hooks of steel.
Hamlet.

26.

TO mourn a mischief that is past and gone
Is the next way to draw new mischief on.
Othello.

27.

EARTHLY power doth then show likest God's,
When mercy seasons justice.
Merchant of Venice.

28.

MEN at some time are masters of their fates.
Julius Cæsar.

29.

IN the great hand of God I stand.
Macbeth.

30.

BE just and fear not.
K. Hen. VIII.

January 31.

A FRIEND should bear his friend's infirmities.
Julius Cæsar.

February 1.

A FEBRUARY face,
So full of frost, of storm, and cloudiness.
Much Ado about Nothing.

2.

NATURE hath framed strange fellows in her time.
Merchant of Venice.

3.

PRAY that the right may thrive.

King Lear.

4.

BE patient till the last.

Julius Cæsar.

5.

WE are such stuff
As dreams are made on, and our little life
Is rounded with a sleep. *Tempest.*

February 6.

MAKE of your prayers one sweet sacrifice,
  And lift my soul to heaven.
               King Henry VIII.

7.

HONOURS thrive
  When rather from our acts we them derive
Than our fore-goers.
         All's Well that Ends Well.

8.

DEFER no time, delays have dangerous ends.
               King Henry VI.

9.

FORTUNE brings in some boats
  that are not steer'd.
               Cymbeline.

10.

SPEAK freely what you think.
               King Henry VI.

11.

A LIGHT heart lives long.
            Love's Labour Lost.

February 12.

COWARDS die many times before their deaths;
The valiant never taste of death but once.
Julius Cæsar.

13.

SHALL we serve Heaven
With less respect than we do minister
To our gross selves? *Measure for Measure.*

14.

HOW far that little candle throws his beams!
So shines a good deed in a naughty world.
Merchant of Venice.

15.

WHAT poor an instrument may do a noble deed.
Antony and Cleopatra.

16.

HE hath a daily beauty in his life.
Othello.

17.

VIRTUE is bold, and goodness never fearful.
Measure for Measure.

February 18.

GOD shall be my hope,
My stay, my guide, and lantern to my feet.
Second Part of King Henry VI.

19.

IN nature there's no blemish but the mind;
None can be called deformed but the unkind.
Twelfth Night.

20.

THERE is no darkness but ignorance.

Twelfth Night.

21.

LET us not burthen our remembrance with
A heaviness that's gone.
Tempest.

22.

BE patient, for the world is broad and wide.
Romeo and Juliet.

23.

LET each man do his best.

First Part of King Henry IV.

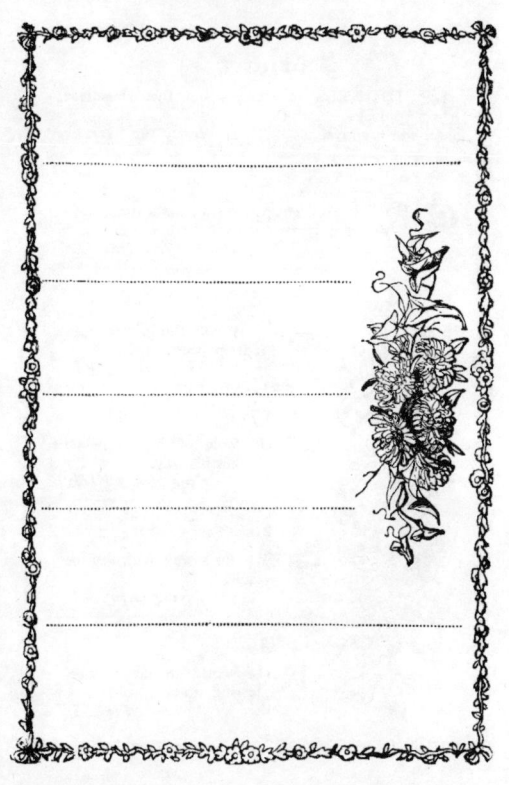

February 24.

KINDNESS in women, not their beauteous looks,
Shall win my love. *Taming of the Shrew.*

25.

OH! it is excellent to have a giant's strength;
But it is tyrannous to use it like a giant.
Measure for Measure.

26.

SAY as you think, and speak it from your souls.
King Henry VI.

27.

THE force of his own merit makes his way.
King Henry VIII.

28.

SEEK for sorrow with thy spectacles.
King Henry VI.

29.

THIS world to me is like a lasting storm.
Pericles.

March 1.

FOR now the wind begins to blow;
Thunder above and deeps below.
Pericles.

2.

PROSPERITY be thy page!

Coriolanus.

3.

WATCH to-night, pray to-morrow.
King Henry IV.

4.

MEN'S evil manners live in brass; their virtues
We write in water.
King Henry VIII.

5.

SILENCE is the perfectest herald of joy.
I were but little happy, if I could say how much. *Much Ado about Nothing.*

6.

WE, ignorant of ourselves, [powers
Beg often our own harms, which the wise
Deny us for our good.

Antony and Cleopatra.

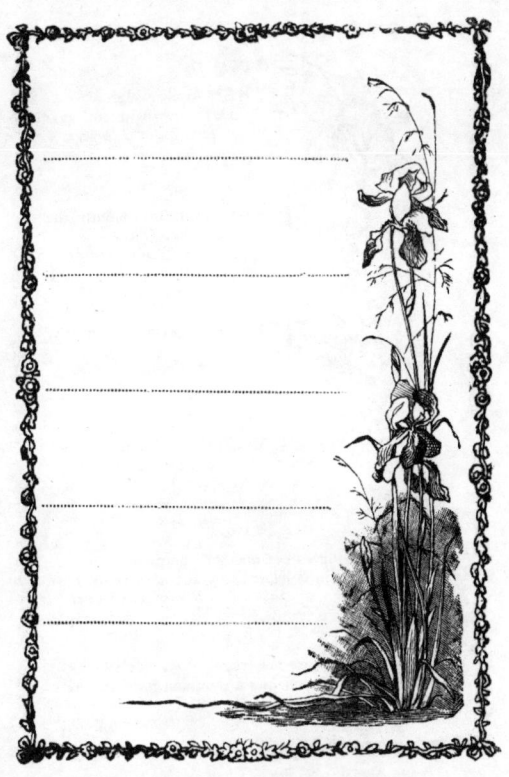

March 7.

THEN wisely weigh
  Our sorrow with our comfort. *Tempest.*

8.

TAKE from my mouth the wish of happy years.
King Richard II.

9.

THE lady is very well worthy.

Much Ado about Nothing.

10.

SMOOTH runs the water where the brook is deep.
King Henry VI., Act iii.

11.

ONE fire burns out another's burning,
  One pain is lessened by another's anguish.
Romeo and Juliet.

12.

OUR praises are our wages: you may ride us
  With one soft kiss a thousand furlongs, ere
With spur we heat an acre.

Winter's Tale.

March 13.

I HAVE heard you say
That we shall see and know our friends in [heaven.
If that be true, I shall see my boy again.
King John.

14.

LOVE sought is good, but given unsought is better.
Twelfth Night.

15.

HE is as full of valour as of kindness.
King Henry V.

16.

LOVE is not love [finds,
Which alters when it alteration
Or bends with the remover to remove.
Sonnet.

17.

AN Irishman, a very valiant gentleman.
King Henry V.

18.

SELF-LOVE is not so vile a sin as self-neglecting.
King Henry V.

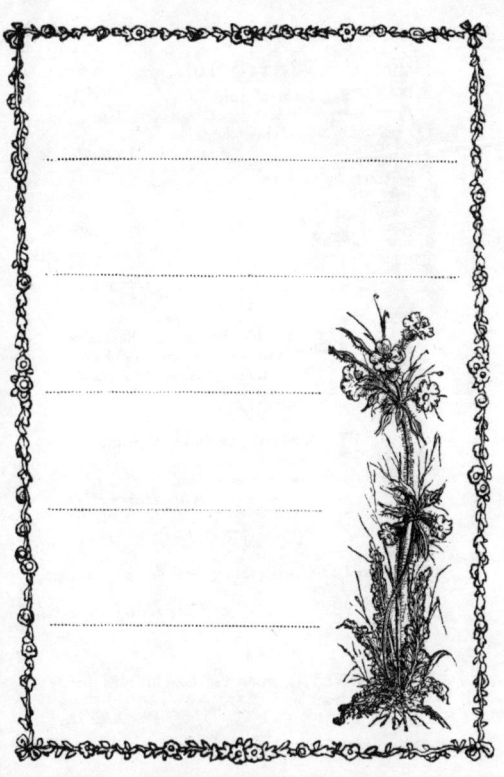

March 19.

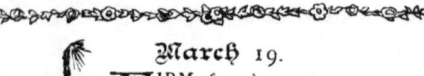

FIRM of word,
 Speaking of deeds and deedless in his tongue.
  Troilus and Cressida.

20.

HIS heart as far from fraud as heaven from earth.
  Two Gentlemen of Verona.

21.

LAY aside life-harming heaviness,
 And entertain a cheerful disposition. *King Richard II.*

22.

I KNOW you have a gentle, noble temper,
A soul as even as a calm.
  King Henry VIII.

23.

EXCEEDING wise, fair-spoken, and persuading.

  King Henry VIII.

24.

CERTAINLY, a woman's thought runs before her actions.
  As You Like It.

March 25.

WE do pray for mercy;
And that same prayer doth teach us all
The deeds of mercy. [to render

Merchant of Venice.

26.

THE rose looks fair, but fairer we it deem
For that sweet odour which doth in it live.

Sonnet.

27.

HIS life was gentle, and the elements
So mix'd in him that Nature might stand up
And say to all the world "This was a man."

Julius Cæsar.

28.

HIS heart and hand both open and both free.

Troilus and Cressida.

29.

ALL that glisters is not gold,
Often have you heard that told.

Merchant of Venice.

30.

HE was my friend, faithful and just to me.

Julius Cæsar.

March 31.

THRICE is he armed that hath his quarrel just;
And he but naked, though locked up in steel,
Whose conscience with injustice is corrupted.
Second Part of King Henry VI.

April 1.

HE jests at scars that never felt a wound.

Romeo and Juliet.

2.

OUR remedies oft in ourselves do lie,
Which we ascribe to Heaven.
All's Well that Ends Well.

3.

HE'S truly valiant that can wisely suffer
The worst that man can breathe.
Timon of Athens.

4.

ALLOW not nature more than nature needs.
King Lear.

5.

THERE'S a special providence in the fall of a sparrow.
Hamlet.

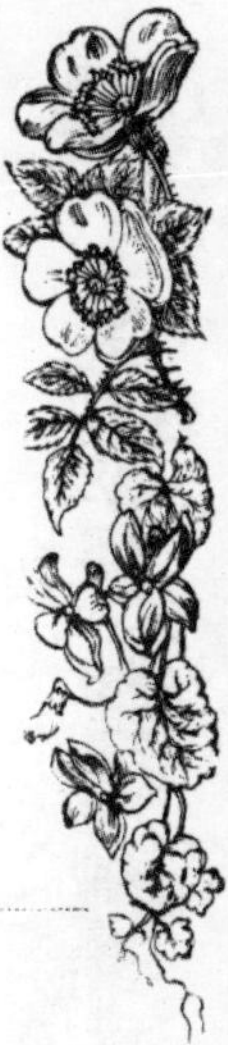

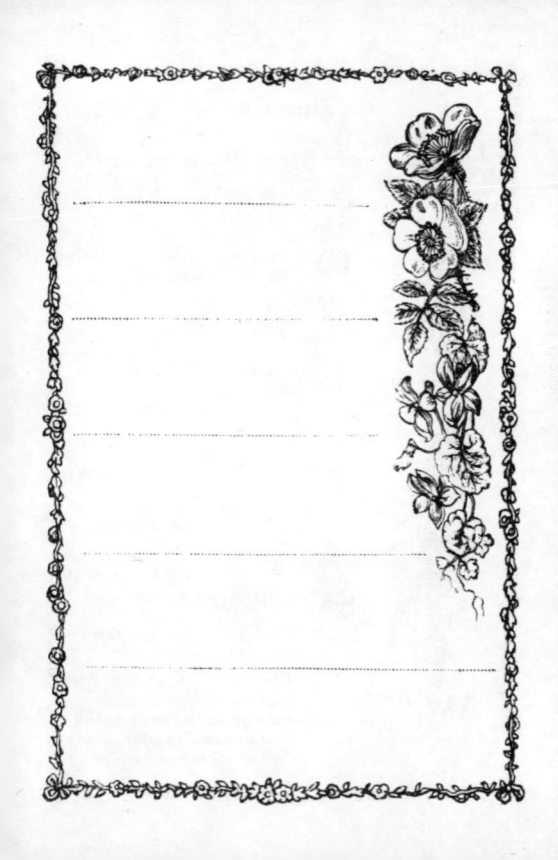

April 6.

COME what come may,
　　Time and the hour runs through the roughest
　　　day.
　　　　　　　　　　　　　　Macbeth.

7.

NO mind that's honest
　　But in it shares some woe.
　　　　　　　　　　　　　　Macbeth.

8.

THE better part of valour is discretion.
　　　　　　　　　　　　　　King Henry IV.

9.

TEACH thy necessity to reason thus;
There is no virtue like necessity.
　　　　　　　　　　　　　　King Richard II.

10.

SUNSHINE and rain at once.

　　　　　　　　　　　　　　King Lear.

11.

WHAT, gone without a word?
　　Ay, so true love should do: it cannot speak;
For truth hath better deeds than words to grace it.
　　　　　　　　　　　　Two Gentlemen of Verona.

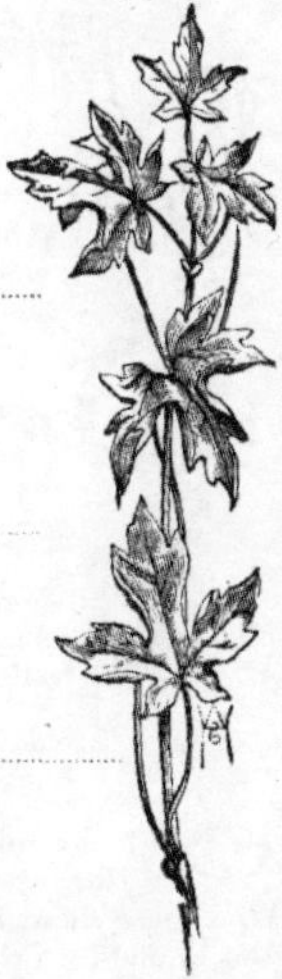

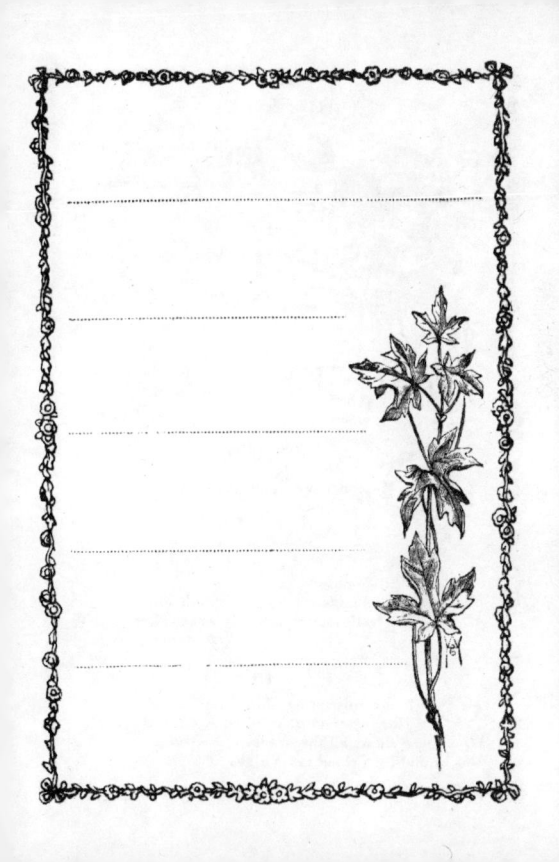

April 12.

HIS life was gentle.

Julius Cæsar.

13.

HOPE is a lover's staff.

Two Gentlemen of Verona.

14.

TRUTH needs no colour, beauty no pencil.

Sonnet.

15.

HE is well paid that is well satisfied.

Merchant of Venice.

16.

LOVE moderately; long love doth so:
Too swift arrives as tardy as too slow.
Romeo and Juliet.

17.

OH! how this spring of love resembleth
　　The uncertain glory of an April day,
Which now shows all the beauty of the sun,
And by-and-by a cloud takes all away!

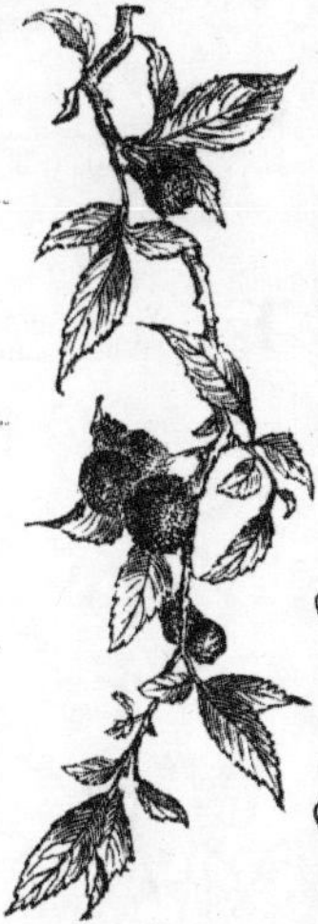

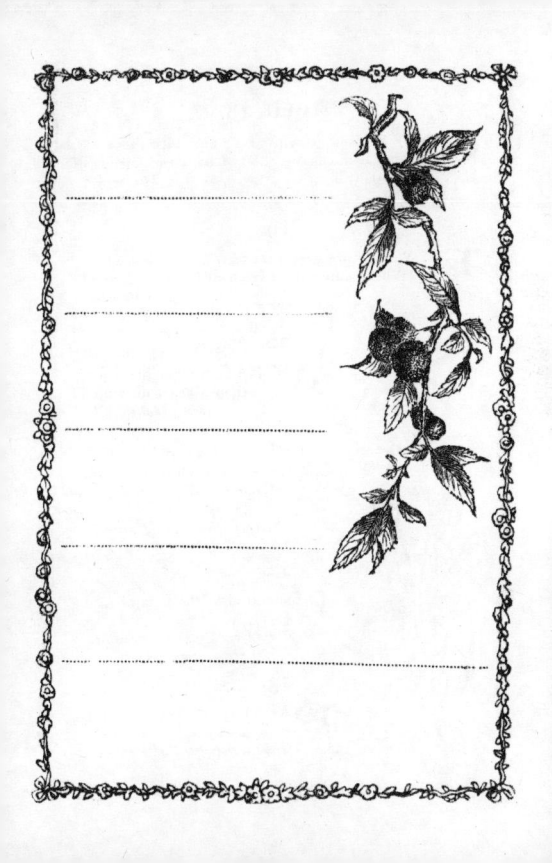

April 18.

GOD'S benison go with you; and with those
That would make good of bad, and friends of
foes.
Macbeth.

19.

HOW poor are they that have not patience!
What wound did ever heal but by degrees?
Othello.

20.

WHAT stronger breastplate
than a heart untainted!
King Henry VI.

21.

SHE excels each mortal thing
Upon the dull earth dwelling.
Two Gentlemen of Verona.

22.

IS she kind as she is fair?

Two Gentlemen of Verona.

23.

PARTING strikes poor lovers
dumb.
Two Gentlemen of Verona.

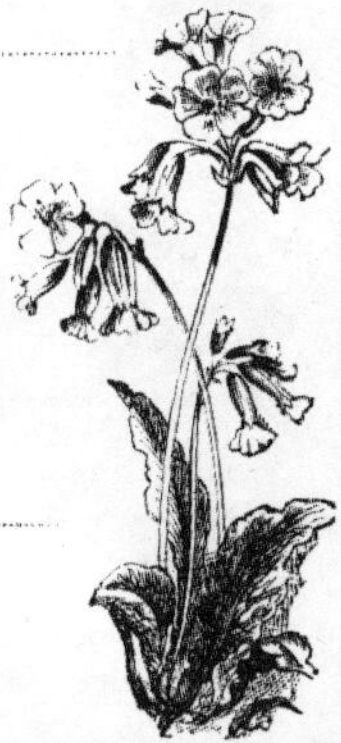

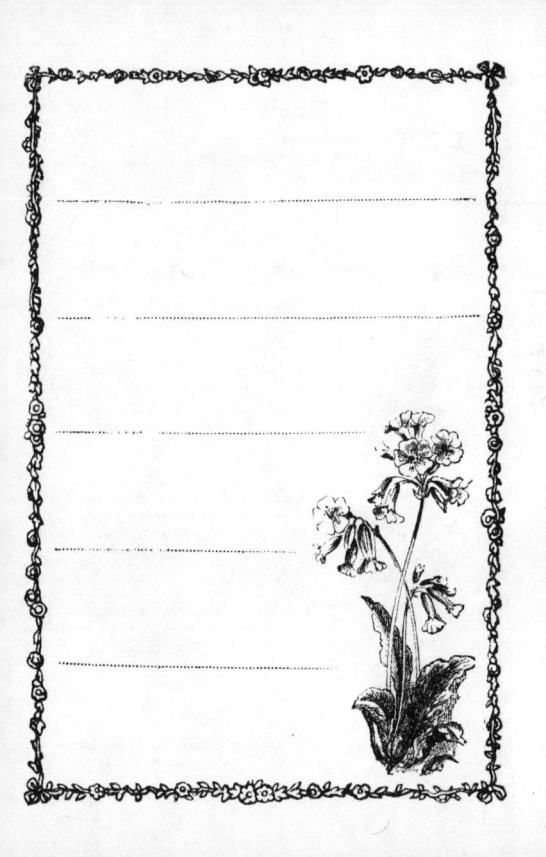

April 24.

BUT we all are men,
   In our own natures frail, and capable
Of our flesh; few are angels.

King Henry VIII.

25.

A MAN whom fortune hath cruelly scratched.

All's Well that Ends Well.

26.

OH! what may man within
   him hide,   [side!
Though angel on the outward
Measure for Measure.

27.

VIRTUE is bold, and
   goodness never fearful.
Measure for Measure.

28.

THE bitter past, more welcome is
   the sweet.
All's Well that Ends Well

29.

THINGS done well,
   And with a care, exempt themselves from fear.
King Henry VIII.

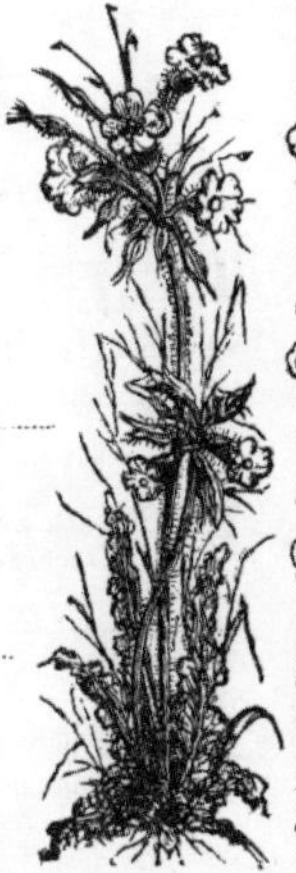

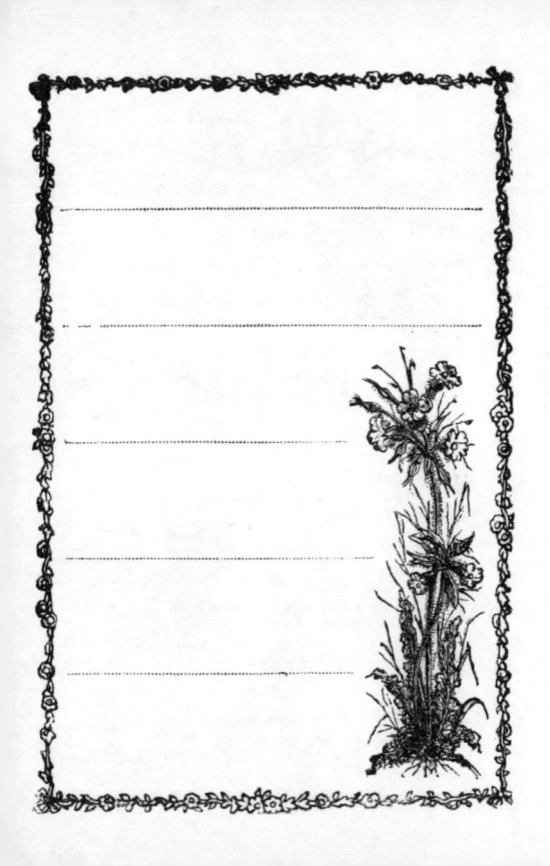

April 30.

A CONSTANT woman.
King Henry VIII.

May 1.

IN beauty as the first of May.
Much Ado about Nothing.

2.

ANGELS are bright still, though the brightest fell.
Macbeth.

3.

THE noblest mind he carries
That ever govern'd man.
Long may he live in fortunes!
Timon of Athens.

4.

HE hath a tear for pity and a hand
Open as day for melting charity.
King Henry IV.

5.

HEAVEN is above all yet; there sits a Judge
That no king can corrupt.
King Henry VIII.

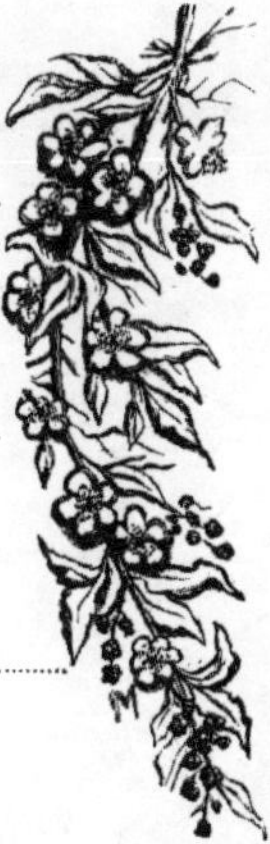

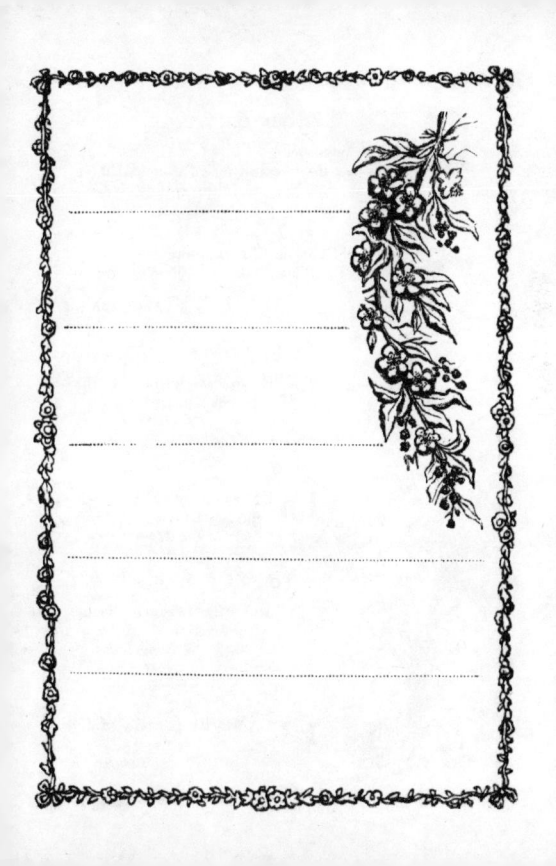

May 6.

HEAVEN bless thee!
Thou hast the sweetest face I ever look'd on.
King Henry VIII.

7.

A VIRTUOUS and a Christian-like conclusion,
To pray for them that have done scathe to us.

King Richard III.

8.

HE sits high in all the people's hearts.
Julius Cæsar.

9.

HER words do show her wit incomparable.
King Henry VI.

10.

STRONG reasons make strong actions.
King John.

11.

BY-AND-BY is easily said.

Hamlet.

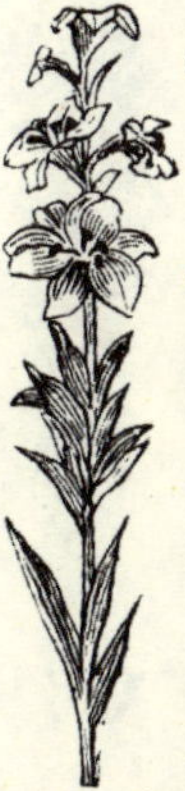

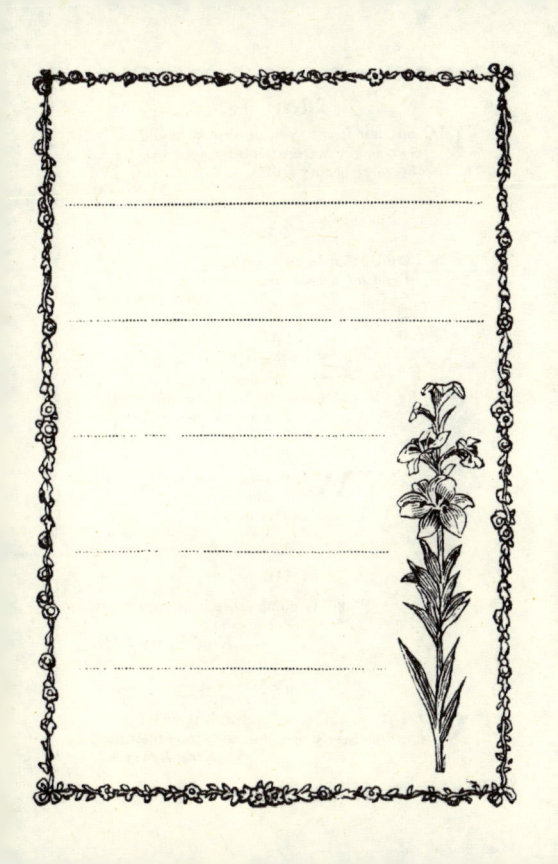

May 12.

To me, fair friend, you never can be old,
  For as you were when first your eye I eyed,
Such seems your beauty still.

Sonnet.

13.

O LORD, that lends me life,
  Lend me a heart replete with thankfulness!
King Henry VI.

14.

EXPERIENCE is by industry achieved
And perfected by the swift course of [time.
Two Gentlemen of Verona.

15.

WE must take the current when it serves,
Or lose our ventures.
Julius Cæsar.

16.

TO climb steep hills requires slow pace at first.
King Henry VIII.

17.

WISE men ne'er sit and wail their loss,
  But cheerly seek how to redress their harms.
King Henry VI.

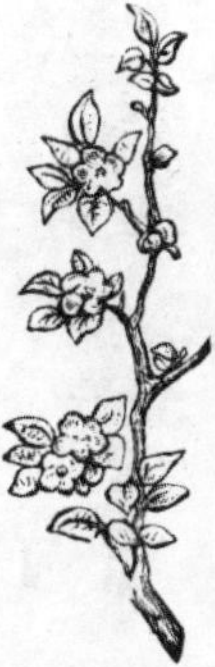

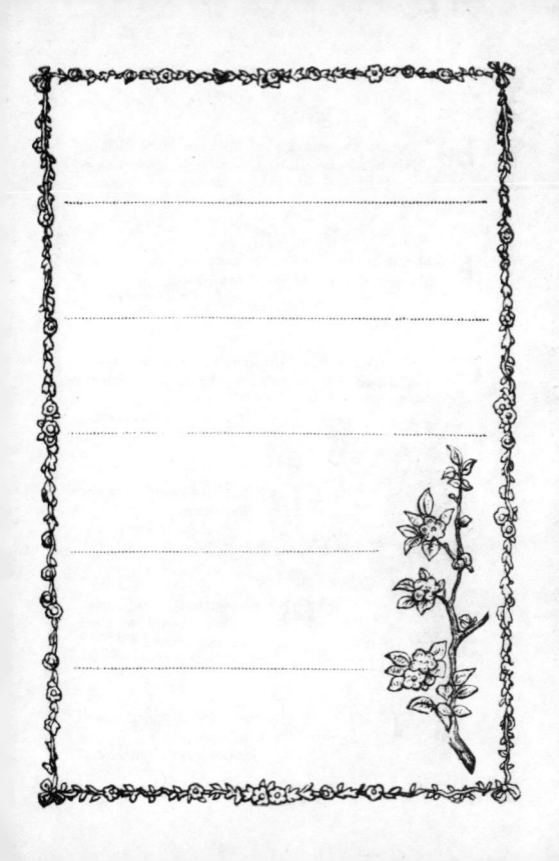

May 18.

His years but young, but his experience old;
His head unmellowed, but his judgment ripe.
Two Gentlemen of Verona.

19.

I AM not of that feather to shake off
My friend when he must need me.
Timon of Athens.

20.

GIVE sorrow words; the grief that does not speak
Whispers the o'erfraught heart and bids it break.
Macbeth.

21.

MEN of few words are the best men.
King Henry V.

22.

BE to yourself [friend.
As you would to your
King Henry VIII.

23.

THEY say best men are moulded out of faults
Measure for Measure.

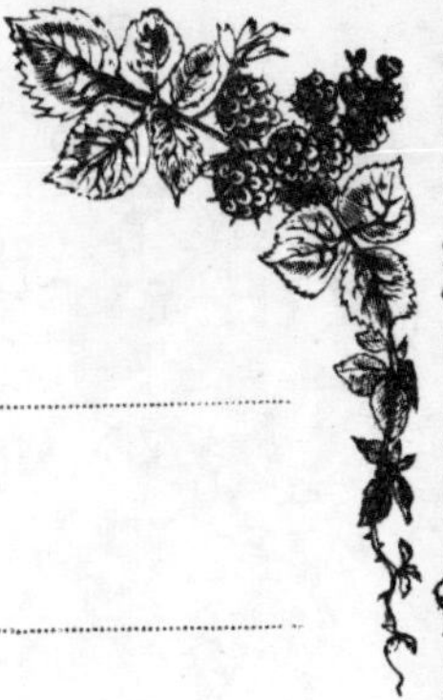

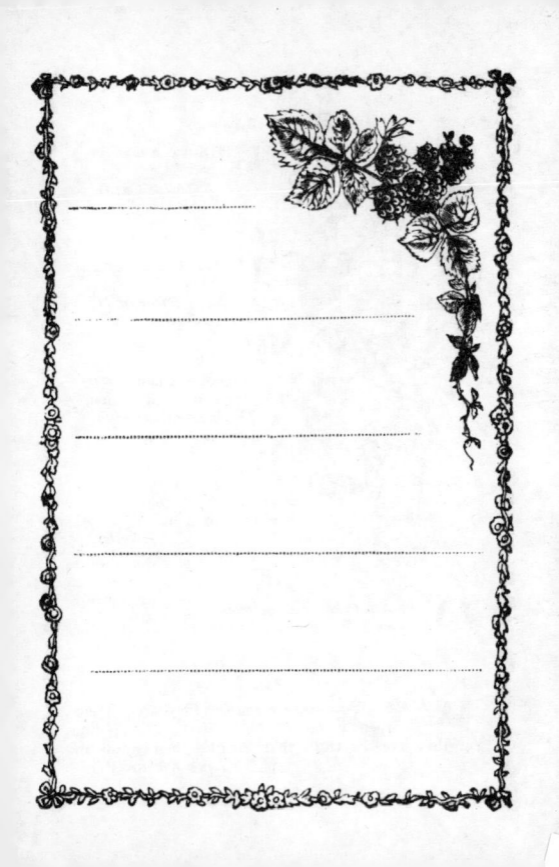

May 24.

THIS was a man.

Julius Cæsar.

25.

TRUTH hath a quiet breast.
King Richard II.

26.

IN the reproof of chance
  Lies the true proof of men.
Troilus and Cressida.

27.

CONFESS yourself to heaven;
Repent what's past; avoid
  what is to come.
Hamlet.

28.

BE cheerful; wipe thine eyes:
  Some falls are means the happier to arise.
Cymbeline.

29.

WHERE words are scarce, they are seldom
  spent in vain, [pain.
For they breathe truth that breathe their words in
King Richard II.

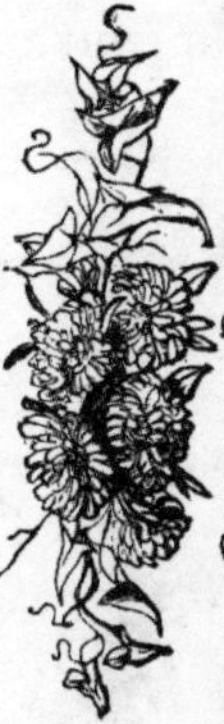

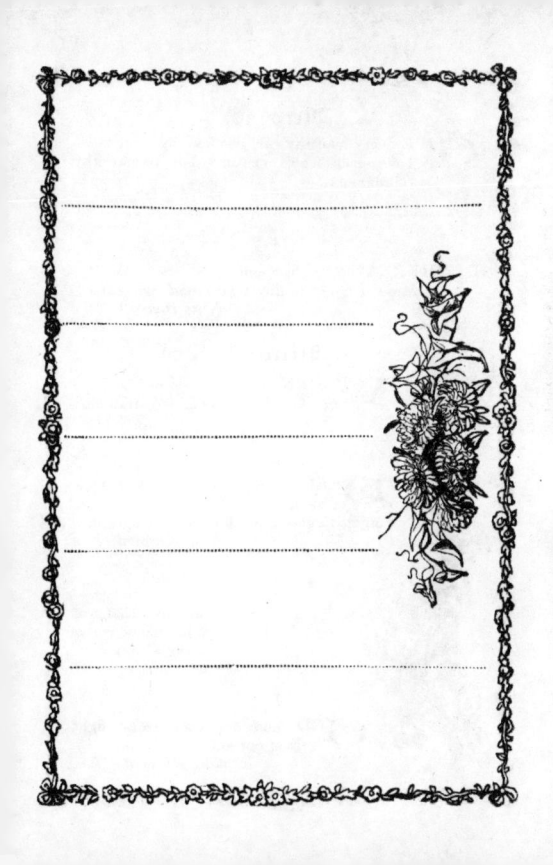

May 30.

GIVE every man thy ear, but few thy voice;
Take each man's censure, but reserve thy judgment.

Hamlet.

31.

THERE is no English soul
More stronger to direct you than yourself.
King Henry VII.

June 1.

WHEN our actions do not,
Our fears do make us traitors.
Macbeth.

2.

DEEP malice makes too deep incision.
Forget, forgive; conclude and be agreed.
King Richard II.

3.

A GOOD heart never changes,
but keeps his course truly.
King Henry V.

4.

GOD and our good cause fight upon our side.
King Richard III.

June 5.

WHAT'S in a name? that which we call a rose
By any other name would smell as sweet.
Romeo and Juliet

6.

HER peerless feature,
Approves her fit for none but for a king
King Henry VI.

7.

I HAVE no other but a woman's reason;
I think him so because I think him so.
Two Gentlemen of Verona.

8.

THE course of true love never did run smooth.

Midsummer Night's Dream

9.

I MUST hear from thee every day i' the hour.
Romeo and Juliet.

10.

'TIS not enough to help the feeble
But to support him after. [up,
Timon of Athens.

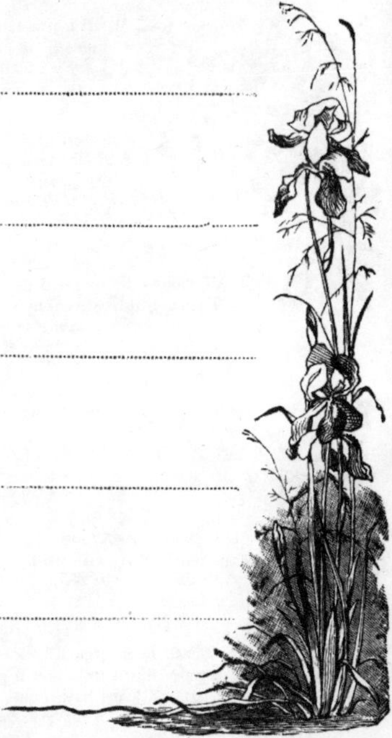

June 11.

SWEET roses in this summer air.
Love's Labour Lost.

12.

GO thou forth,
And fortune play upon thy prosperous helm.
All's Well that Ends Well.

13.

WHAT cannot be avoided [or fear.
'Twere childish weakness to lament
King Henry VI.

14.

EVERY one can master a grief but he that has it.
Much Ado About Nothing.

15.

IGNORANCE is the curse of God,
Knowledge the wing wherewith we fly to heaven.
Second Part of King Henry VI.

16.

GOD'S goodness hath been great to thee:
Let never day nor night unhallow'd pass,
But still remember what the Lord hath done.
King Henry VI.

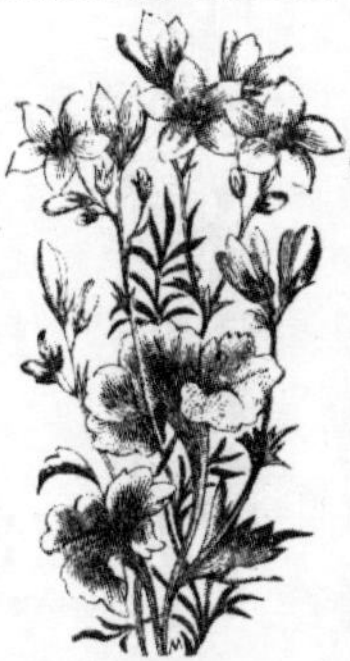

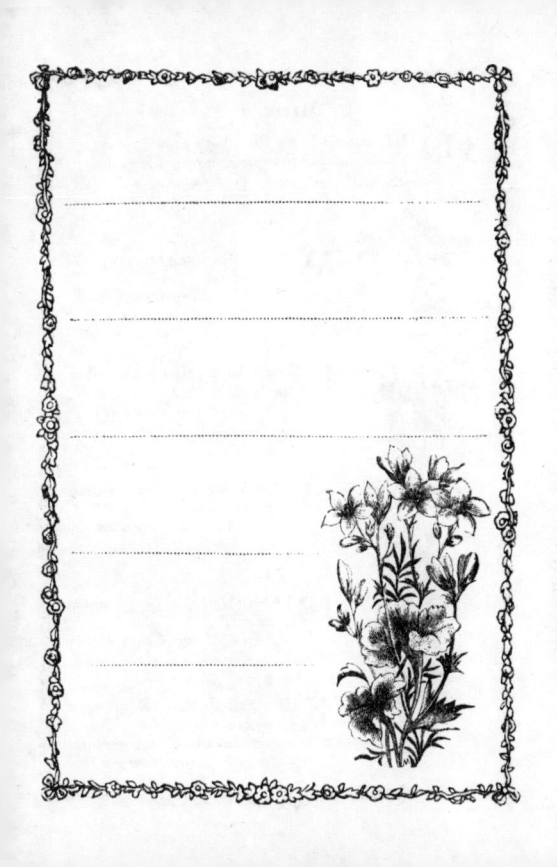

June 17.

MINE honour is my life; both grow in one;
Take honour from me, and my life is done.
King Richard II.

18.

WATCH to-night, pray to-morrow.
King Henry IV.

19.

I MUST have patience to endure the load.
King Richard III.

20.

ALLOW not nature more than nature needs.
King Lear.

21.

BLESSED are the peacemakers on earth.
King Henry VI.

22.

THE trust I have is in mine innocence,
And therefore am I bold and resolute.
King Henry VI.

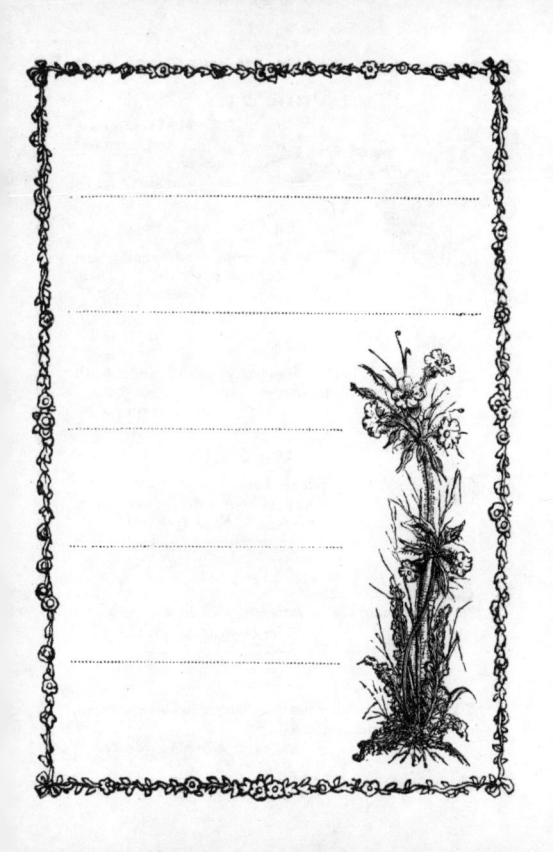

June 23

A MAID of grace,
And complete majesty.
Love's Labour Lost.

24.

WHAT'S gone and what's past
Should be past grief.
Winter's Tale.

25.

THE strawberry grows underneath the nettle.
King Henry V.

26.

MANY days shall see her,
And yet no day without a deed to crown it.
King Henry VIII.

27.

SHE looks as clear
As morning roses newly washed with dew.
Taming of the Shrew.

28.

THE means that heaven yields must be embraced,
And not neglected.
King Richard II.

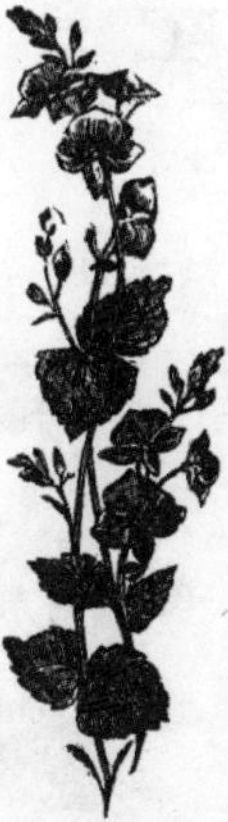

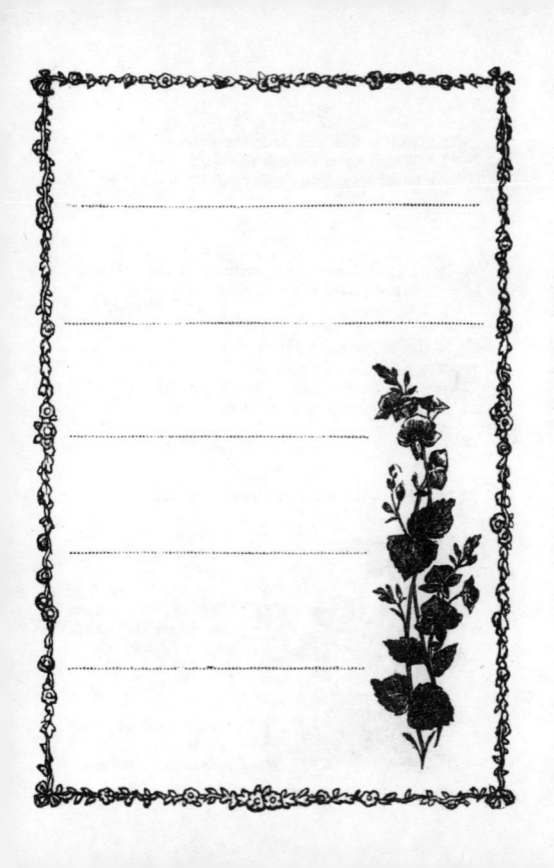

June 29.

GLORY is like a circle in the water,
  Which never ceaseth to enlarge itself,
Till, by broad spreading, it disperse to nought.
King Henry VI.

30.

PRINCES have but their titles for their glories,
  An outward honour for an inward toil.
King Richard III.

July 1.

TO thine own self be true,
  And it must follow, as the night the day,
Thou canst not then be false to any man.

Hamlet.

2.

ILL blows the wind that profits nobody.

King Henry VI.

3.

FORBEAR to judge, for we are sinners all.
King Henry VI.

4.

PATCH grief with proverbs.
Much Ado about Nothing.

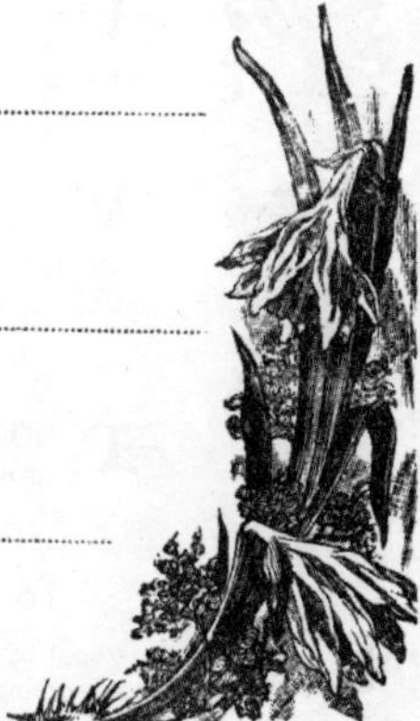

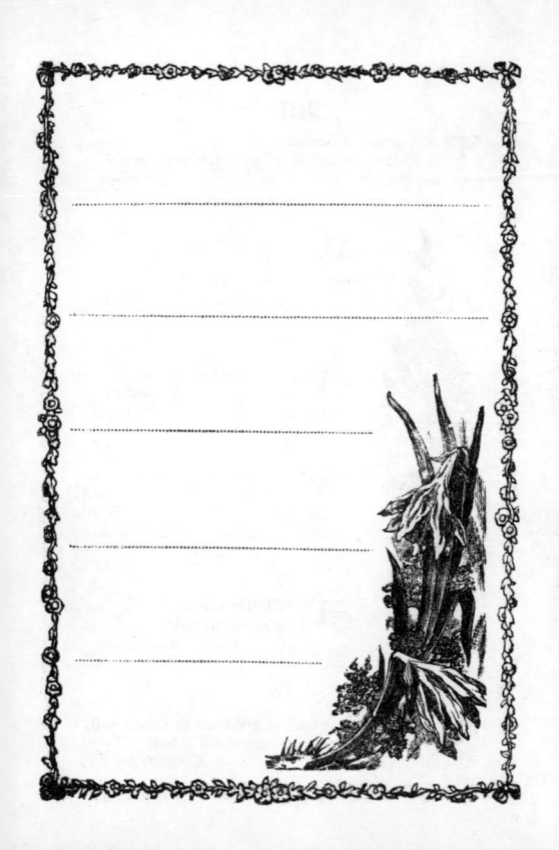

July 5.

THE grace of heaven,
 Before, behind thee, and on every hand,
Enwheel thee round! *Othello.*

6.

WHAT'S brave, what's noble,
 Let's do it . . .
And make death proud to take us.
Antony and Cleopatra.

7.

ALL that lives must die,
 Passing through nature to eternity. *Hamlet.*

8.

WE bring forth weeds
 When our quick minds lie still.
Antony and Cleopatra.

9.

A GOOD man's fortune may grow out at heels.
King Lear.

10.

THERE is some soul of goodness in things evil,
 Would men observingly distil it out.
King Henry V.

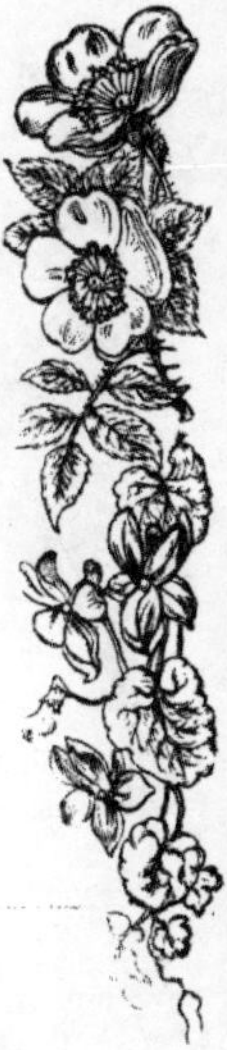

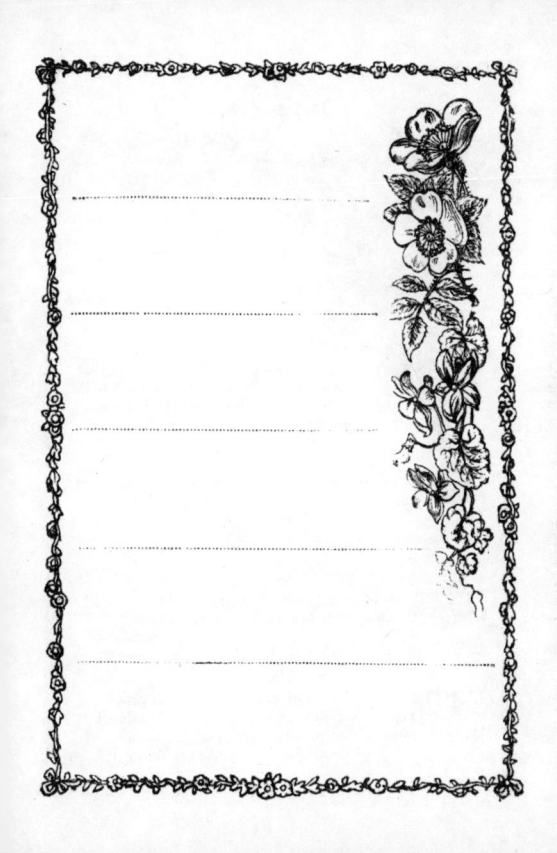

July 11.

GOD is our fortress.
King Henry VI.

12.

NEVER anger Made good guard for itself.
Antony and Cleopatra.

13.

AND he wants wit that wants resolved will.
Two Gentlemen of Verona.

14.

BETTER a little chiding than a great deal of heart-break.
Merry Wives of Windsor.

15.

FOR where is any author in the world
Teaches such beauty as a woman's eye?
Love's Labour Lost.

16.

'**T**IS beauty that doth oft make women proud,
'Tis virtue that doth make them most admired;
'Tis government that makes them seem divine.
King Henry VI.

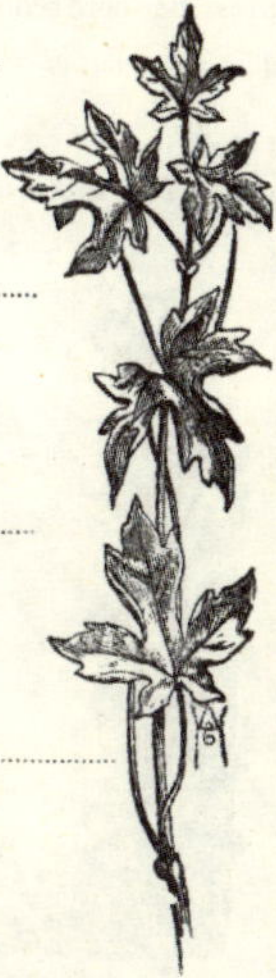

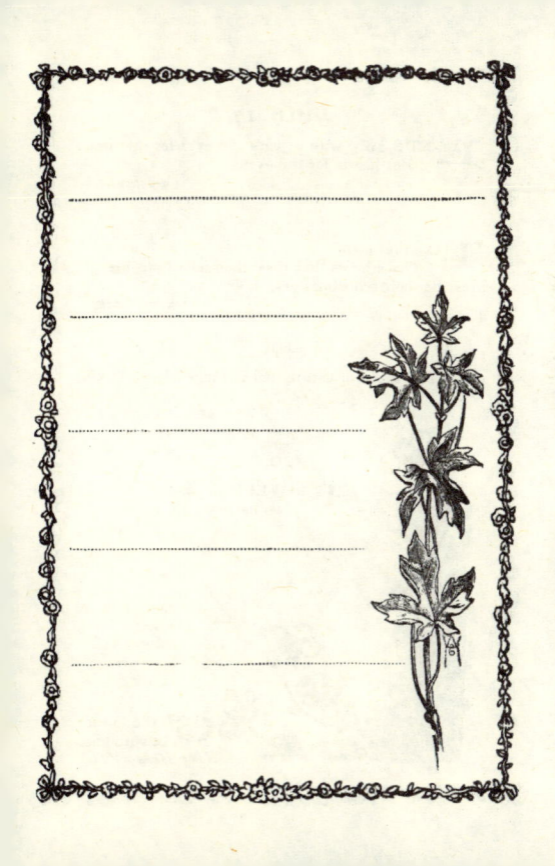

July 17.

LET'S carry with us ears and eyes for the time.
But hearts for the event.

Coriolanus.

18.

TO wilful men,
The injuries that they themselves procure
Must be their schoolmasters.

King Lear.

19.

ONE touch of nature makes the whole world kin.

Troilus and Cressida.

20.

A LOVELY union—
Two berries on a bough.

Sonnet.

21.

LET each man do his best.
King Henry IV.

22.

GOD'S peace be with him
King Henry VIII.

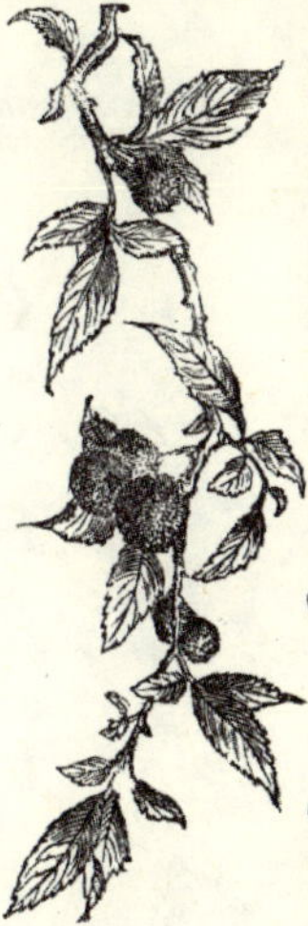

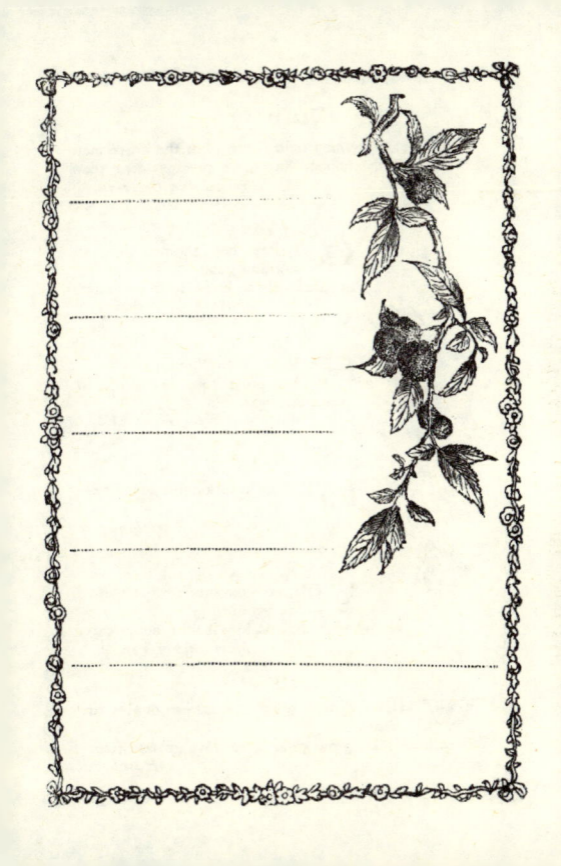

July 23.

LIFE every man holds dear; but the brave man Holds honour far more precious-dear than life. *Troilus and Cressida.*

24.

LET me be ignorant, and in nothing good,
But graciously to know I am no better.
Measure for Measure.

25.

FAIR be all thy hopes,
And prosperous be thy life, in peace and war.
King Henry VI.

26.

HE shall have a noble memory.

Coriolanus.

27.

YOU have too much respect upon the world:
They lose it that do buy it with much care.
Merchant of Venice.

28.

WHERE love is great the littlest doubts are fears;
Where little fears grow great, great love grows there.
Hamlet.

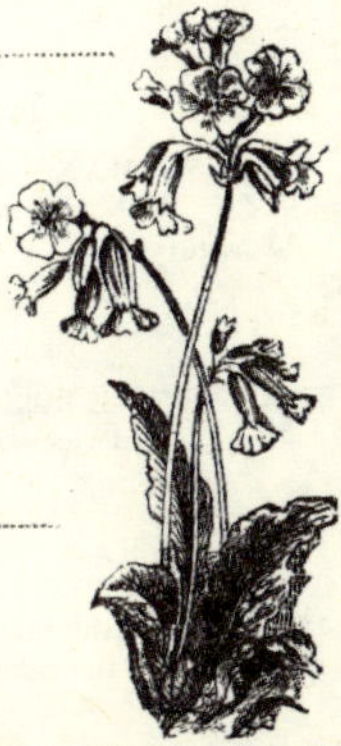

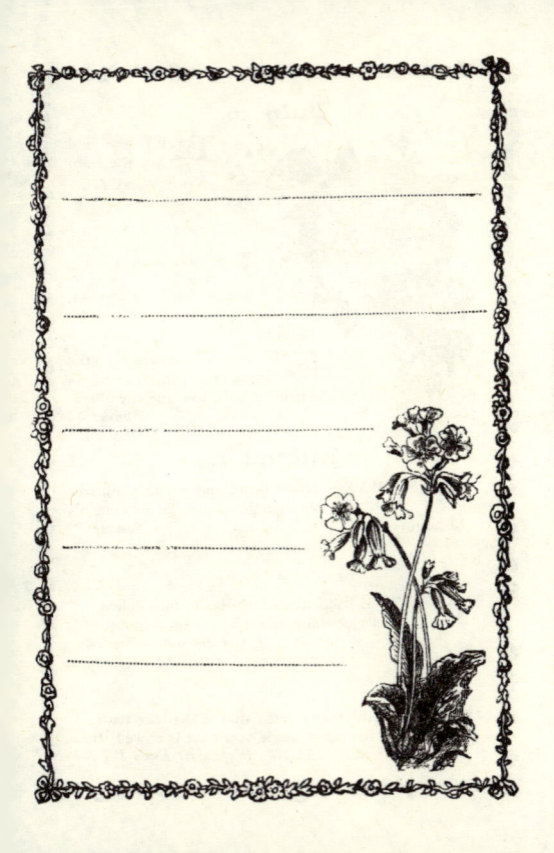

July 29.

LET the end try the man.
King Henry IV.

30.

IS she not passing fair?
Two Gentlemen of Verona.

31.

THE summer's flower is to the summer sweet,
Though to itself it only live and die.
Sonnet.

August 1.

A WOMAN'S gentle heart, but not acquainted
With shifting change, as is false women's fashion.
Sonnet.

2.

VIRTUE itself turns vice, being misapplied;
And vice sometime's by action dignified.
Romeo and Juliet.

3.

'**T**IS not the many oaths that makes the truth,
But the plain single vow that is vowed true.
All's Well that Ends Well.

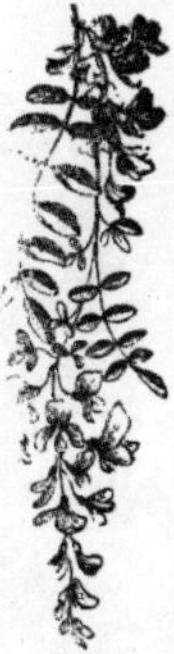

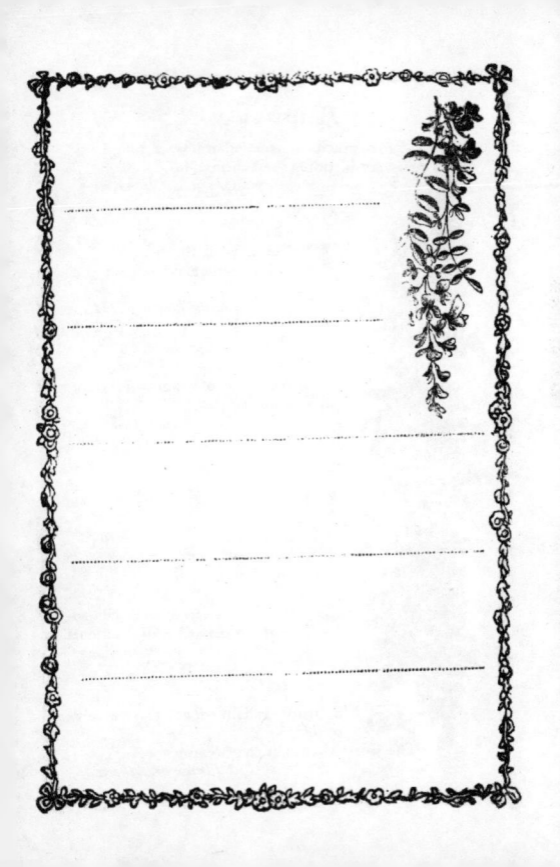

August 4.

GIVE to a gracious message an host of tongues;
But let ill tidings tell themselves.
Antony and Cleopatra.

5.

THERE is no English soul
More stronger to direct you than yourself.
King Henry VIII.

6.

IN delay
We waste our lights in vain, like lamps by day.
Romeo and Juliet.

7.

POWERS divine behold our human actions.
Winter's Tale.

8.

SHE is of so free, so kind, so apt, so blessed a disposition.
Othello.

9.

HE'S truly valiant that can wisely suffer
The worst that man can breathe.
Timon of Athens.

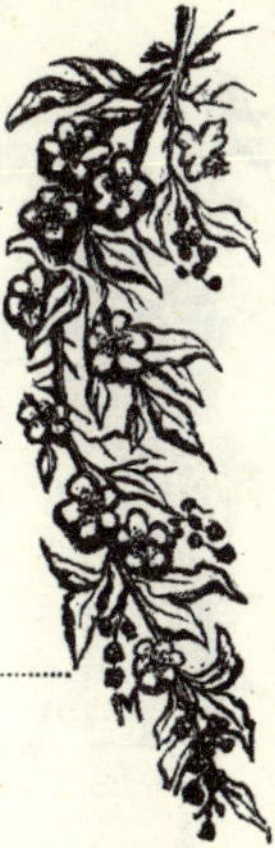

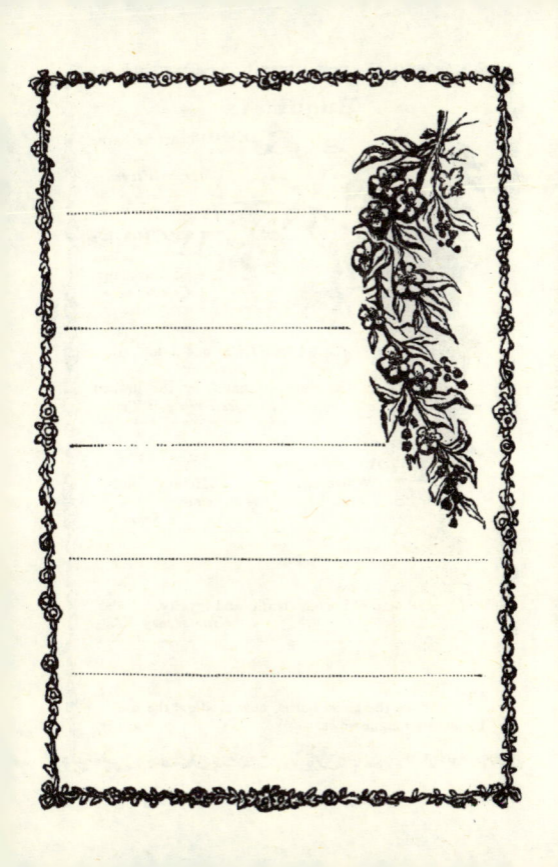

August 10.

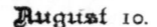

A KIND heart he hath.

Merry Wives.

11.

WHO is't can read a woman?
Cymbeline.

12.

OPINION'S but a fool, that makes us scan
The outward habit by the inward man. *Pericles Prince of Tyre.*

13.

LOVE is not love
Which alters when it alteration finds,
Or bends with the remover to remove.
Sonnet.

14.

IN thy face I see
The map of honour, truth, and loyalty.
King Henry VI.

15.

I DO know,
When the blood burns, how prodigal the soul
Lends the tongue vows. *Hamlet.*

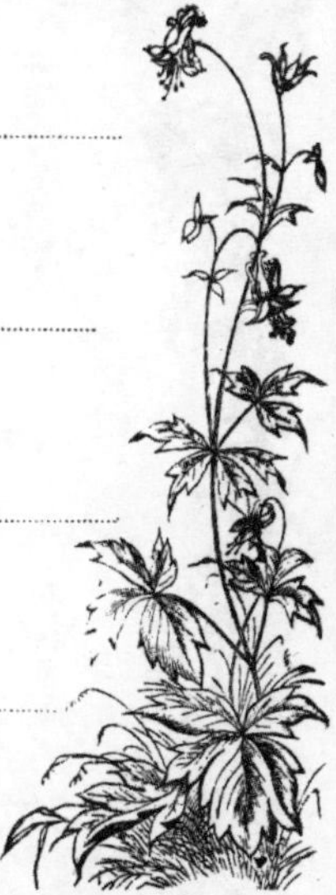

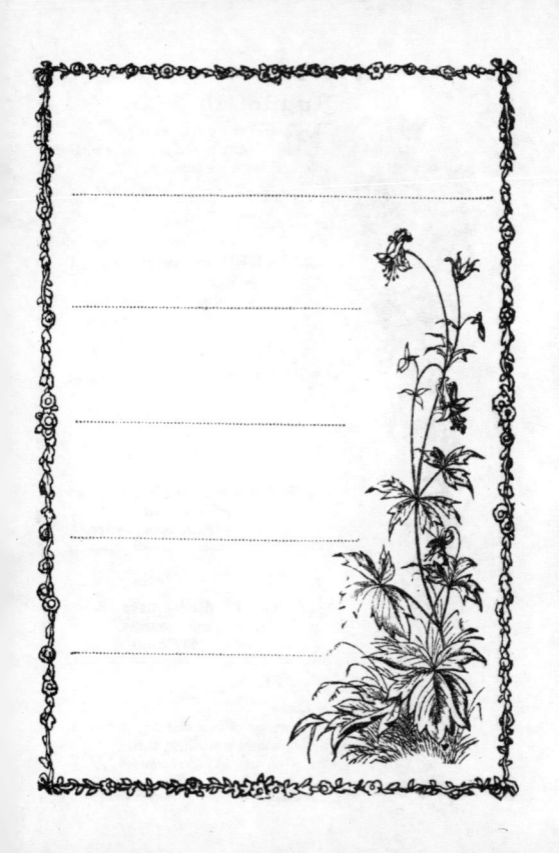

August 16

HER voice was ever soft,
    Gentle, and low, an excellent thing in woman.
King Lear.

17.

SACRED and sweet was all I saw in her.
Taming of the Shrew.

18.

YOUTH, the more it is wasted the sooner it wears.
King Henry IV.

19.

WHERE care lodges, sleep will never lie.
Romeo and Juliet.

20.

GREAT floods have flown from simple sources.
All's Well that Ends Well.

21.

ALL of us have cause
    To wail the dimming of our shining star
But none can cure their harms by wailing them.
King Richard III.

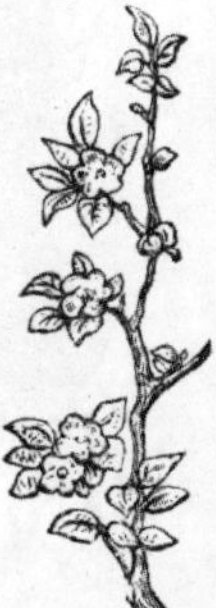

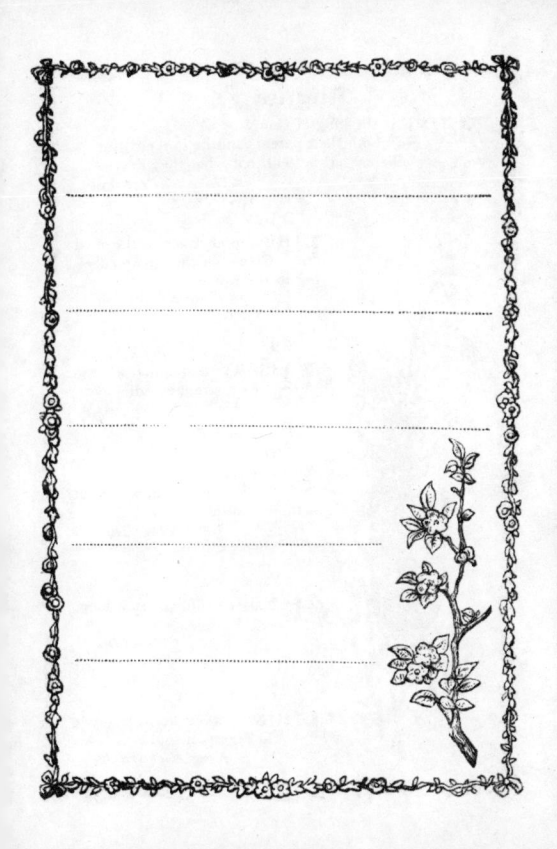

August 22.

TIME is the king of men,
 He's both their parent, and he is their grave,
And gives them what he will, not what they crave.
Pericles.

23.

THE apprehension of the good
 Gives but the greater feeling to the worse.
King Richard II.

24.

MISERY acquaints a man
 with strange bedfellows.
Tempest.

25.

MEN must endure
 Their going hence, even as their coming hither.
King Lear.

26.

A NOBLE life before a long.

Coriolanus.

27.

THINGS sweet to taste prove
 in digestion sour.
King Richard II.

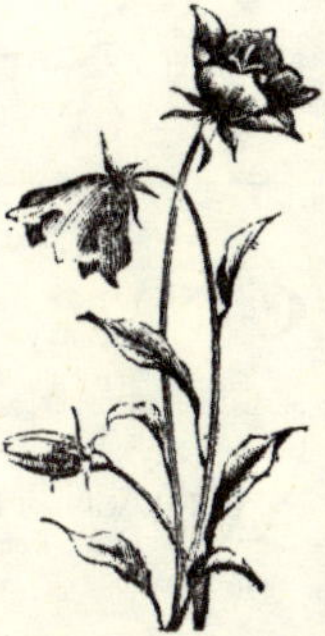

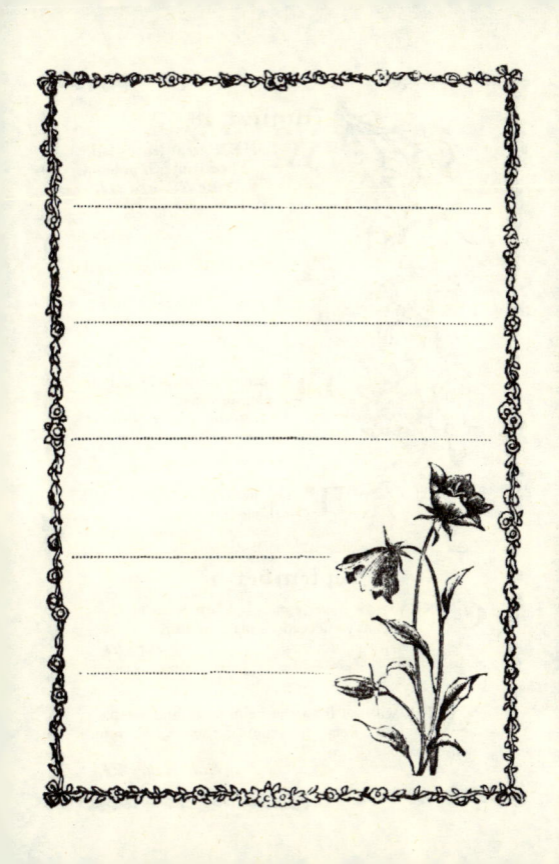

August 28.

WHEN great leaves fall,
Then winter is at hand.
King Richard III.

29.

A GRACIOUS innocent soul.

Winter's Tale.

30.

NO profit grows where is no pleasure ta'en.
Taming of the Shrew.

31.

THE heavens speed thee in thine enterprise.
Julius Cæsar.

September 1.

ONE sorrow never comes but brings an heir,
That may succeed as his inheritor.

Pericles.

2.

WE will not from the helm to sit and weep,
But keep our course, though the rough wind say no.

King Henry VI.

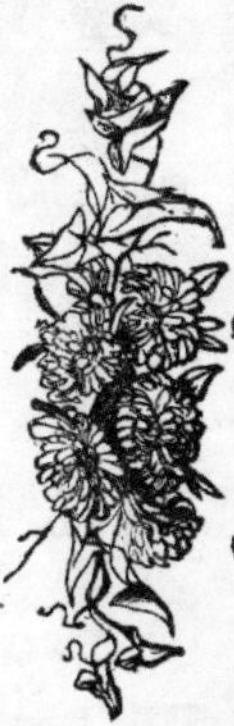

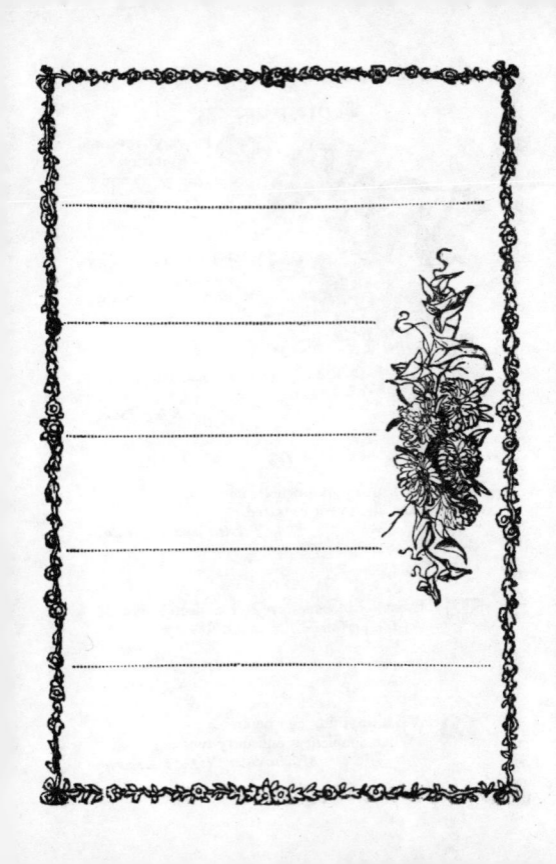

September 3.

OF very reverend reputation.
Comedy of Errors

4.

SWEET mercy is nobility's true badge.
Titus Andronicus.

5.

HE hath a stern look, but a gentle heart.
King John.

6.

FAIR fruit in an unwholesome dish
Are like to rot untasted.
Troilus and Cressida.

7.

THE canker-blooms have full as deep a dye
As the perfumed tincture of the roses.
Sonnet.

8.

NEVER anything can be amiss,
When simpleness and duty tender it
Midsummer Night's Dream.

September 9.

WHEN remedies are past, the griefs are ended
By seeing the worst, which late on hopes depended.
Othello.

10.

HAPPY thou art not;
For what thou hast not, still thou striv'st to get,
And what thou hast, forget'st.
Measure for Measure.

11.

LIGHT boats sail swift, though greater hulks draw deep.
Troilus and Cressida.

12.

A WOMAN'S face with Nature's own hand painted.
Sonnet.

13.

THERE'S nothing ill can dwell in such a temple. *Tempest.*

14.

WIN straying souls,
Cast none away.
Henry VIII.

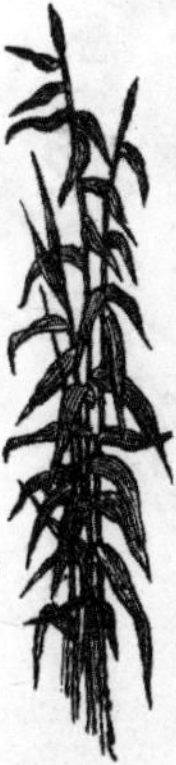

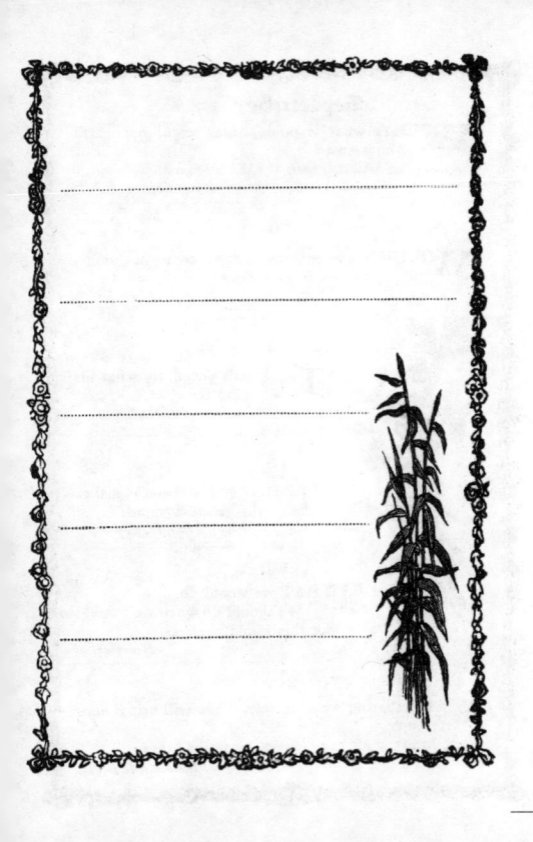

September 15.

WHY, what is pomp, rule, reign, but earth and dust?
And, live we how we can, yet die we must.
King Henry VI.

16.

WHEN sorrows come, they come not single spies, but in battalions!
Hamlet.

17.

HE tells you flatly what his mind is.
Taming of the Shrew.

18.

THE empty vessel makes the greatest sound.
King Henry V.

19.

THAT we would do,
We should do when we would; for this would changes.
Hamlet.

20.

BE suffering what it may, Time will bring summer,
When briars shall have leaves, as well as thorns,
And be as sweet as sharp. —*All's Well that Ends Well.*

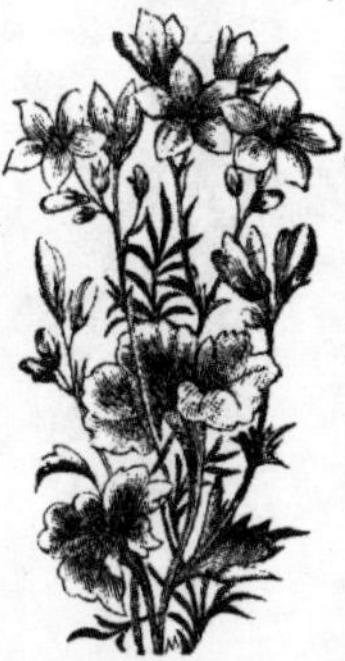

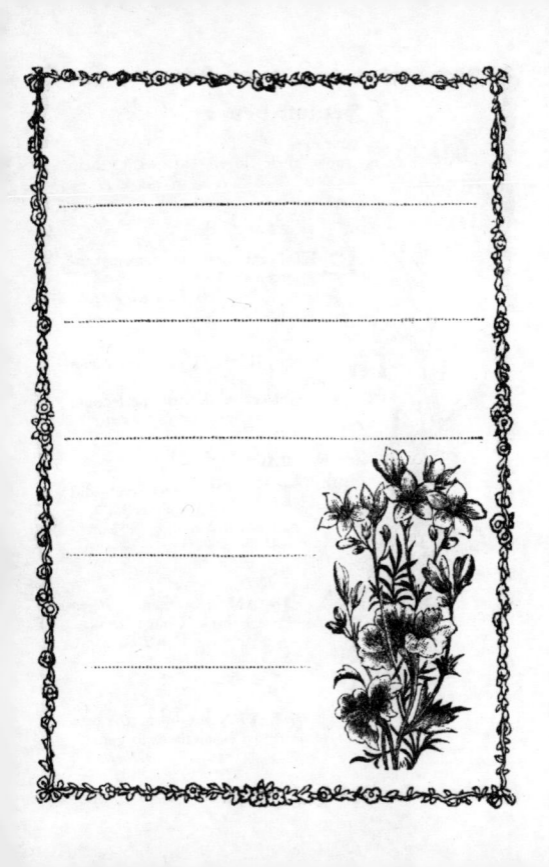

September 21.

DAY, dry your eyes:
  Tears show their love, but want their remedies.
  King Richard II.

22.

LET gentleness my strong enforcement be!
  As You Like It.

23.

HOW many things by season season'd are
To their right praise and true perfection.
  Merchant of Venice.

24.

DUTY never yet did want his meed.
  Two Gentlemen of Verona.

25.

I AM a woman. When I think, I must speak.
  As You Like It.

26.

MEN are men; the best sometimes forget.
  Othello.

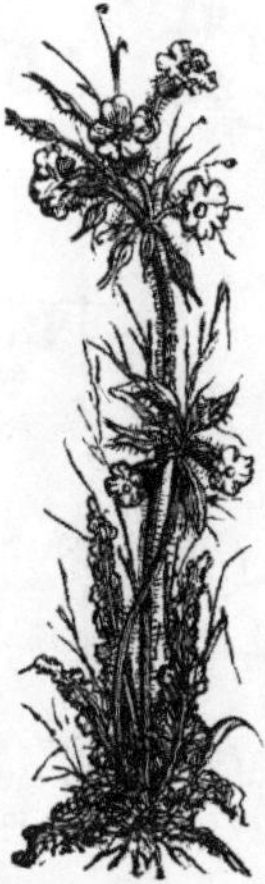

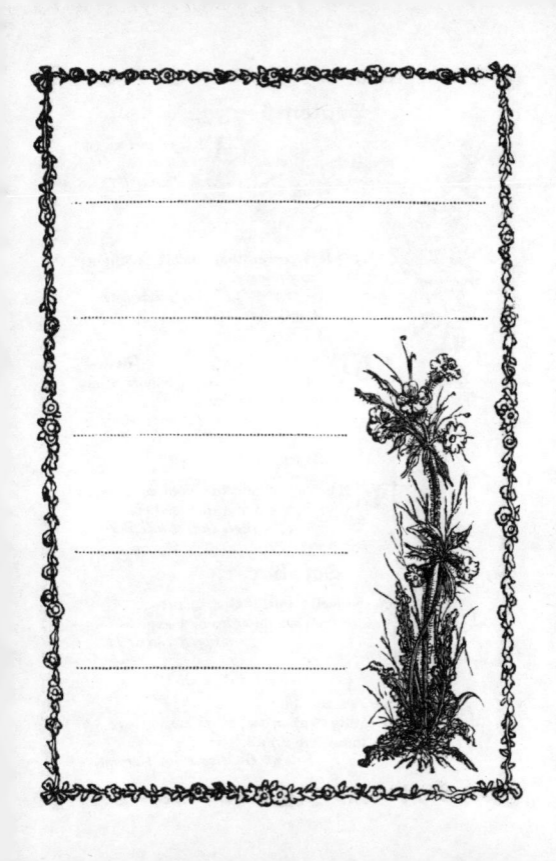

September 27.

ALL is best as 'tis.

King Richard II.

28.

THE power that makes is mighty to preserve.

King Richard II.

29.

MY endeavours [desires,
Have ever come too short of my
Yet filled with my abilities.

King Henry VIII.

30.

THE web of our life is of a mingled yarn, good and ill together.

All's Well that Ends Well.

October 1.

ALL may be well; but, if God sort it so,
'Tis more than we deserve, or I expect.

King Richard III.

2.

AS in the sweetest bud
The eating canker dwells, so eating love
Inhabits in the finest wits of all.

Two Gentlemen of Verona.

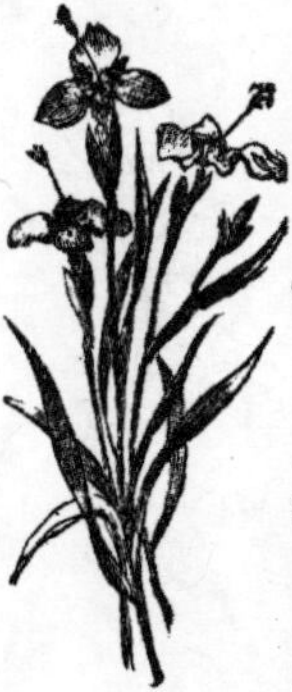

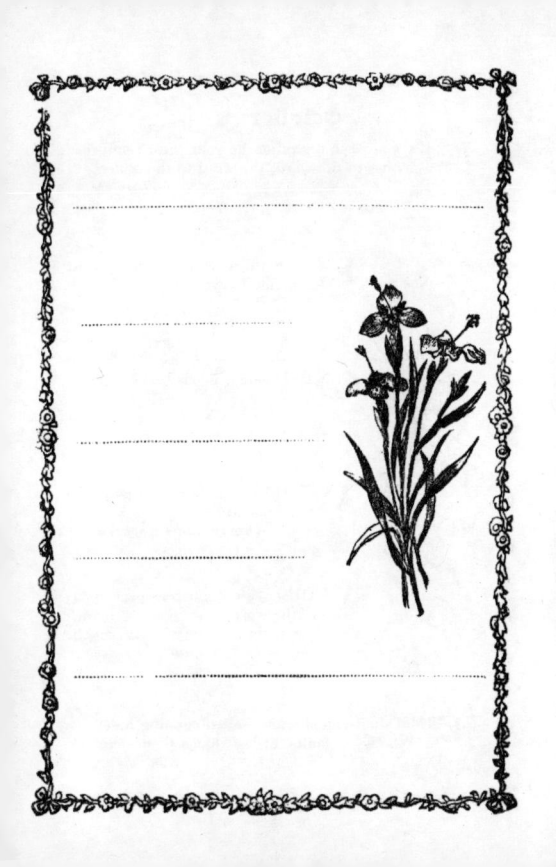

October 3.

LET your own discretion be your tutor: suit the action to the word, the word to the action.
Hamlet.

4.

HE hath a wisdom that doth guide his valour.
Macbeth.

5.

OUR content is our best having.
King Henry VIII.

6.

WHAT Providence delays it not denies.
Antony and Cleopatra.

7.

YOU have too much respect upon the world: [care.
They lose it that do buy it with much
Merchant of Venice.

8.

TIME shall unfold what plaited cunning hides:
Who cover faults, at last shame them derides.
King Lear.

....

....

....

....

....

October 9.

BY a divine instinct, men's minds mistrust
    Ensuing dangers; as, by proof, we see
The waters swell before a boisterous storm.
But leave it all to God. *King Richard III.*

10.

VIRTUE and genuine graces in themselves
    Speak what no words can utter.
                    Antony and Cleopatra.

11.

IN the modesty of fearful duty
    I read as much as from the rattling tongue
Of saucy and audacious eloquence.
                    Midsummer Night's Dream

12.

A LOYAL, just, and upright gentleman.

                    King Richard II.

13.

TORCHES were made
    to burn.
                    Sonnet.

14.

FLING away ambition.

                    King Henry VIII.

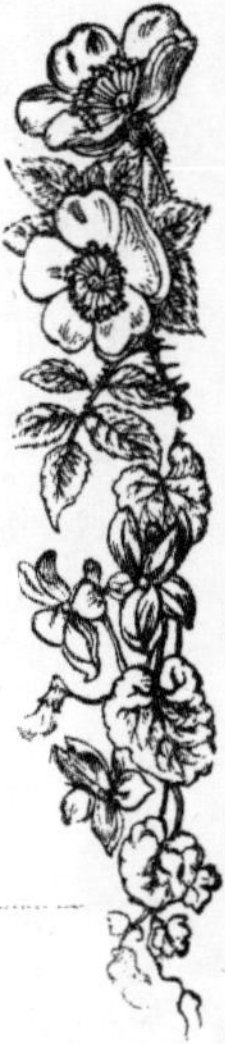

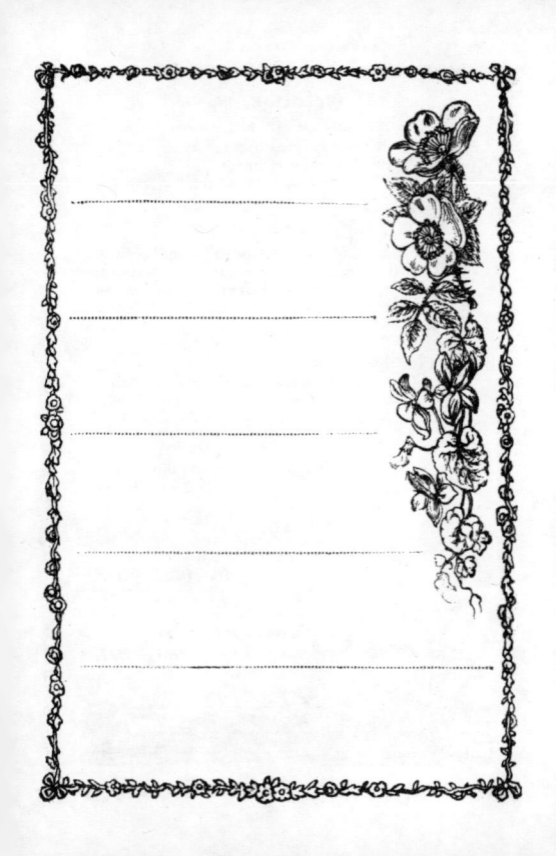

October 15.

HE is the half part of a blessed man,
  Left to be finished by such as she;
And she a fair divided excellence,
Whose fulness of perfection lies in him.— *King John.*

16.

HIS tears pure messengers sent from his heart,
  His heart as far from fraud as heaven from earth. *Two Gentlemen of Verona.*

17.

GIVE thy thoughts no tongue,
  Nor any unproportioned thought his act.
  Hamlet.

18.

HOW full of briers is this working-day world!
  As You Like It.

19.

TO fear the worst oft cures the worse.
  Troilus and Cressida.

20.

GOOD grows with her.
  King Henry VIII.

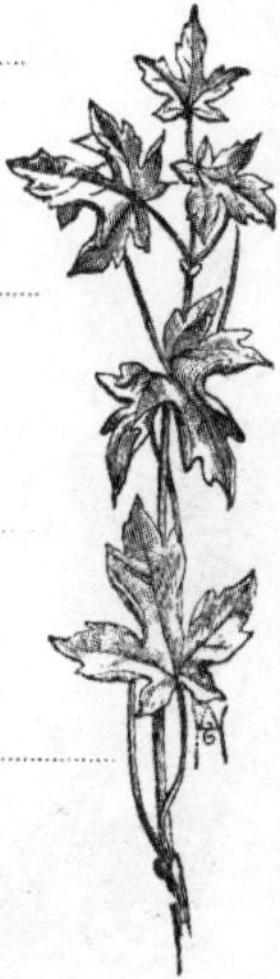

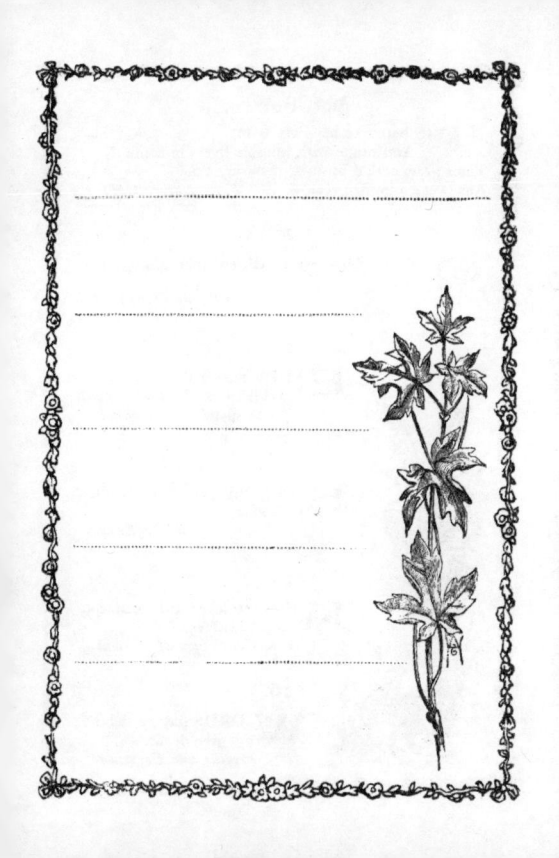

October 21.

'TIS better to be lowly born,
  And range with humble livers in content,
Than to be perk'd up in a glistering grief
And wear a golden sorrow. *King Henry VIII.*

22.

O THE fierce wretchedness that glory brings us!
Timon of Athens.

23.

EVERY man will be thy friend
  Whilst thou hast wherewith
   to spend. *Sonnet.*

24.

KEEP thy pen from lenders' books.
King Lear.

25.

HE never loved that can conceal his love.
Two Gentlemen of Verona.

26.

WORDS pay no debts;
  give deeds.
Troilus and Cressida.

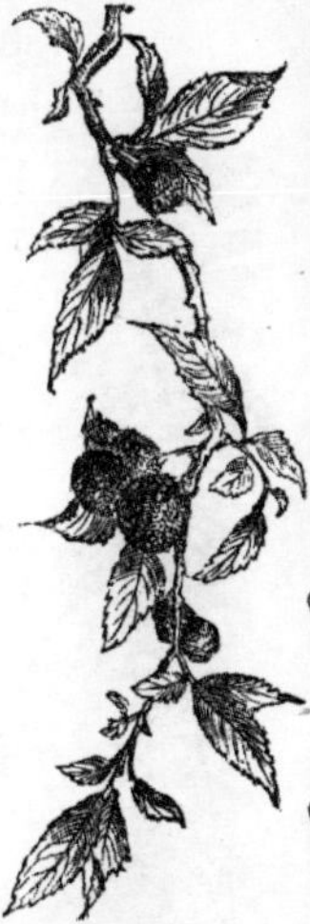

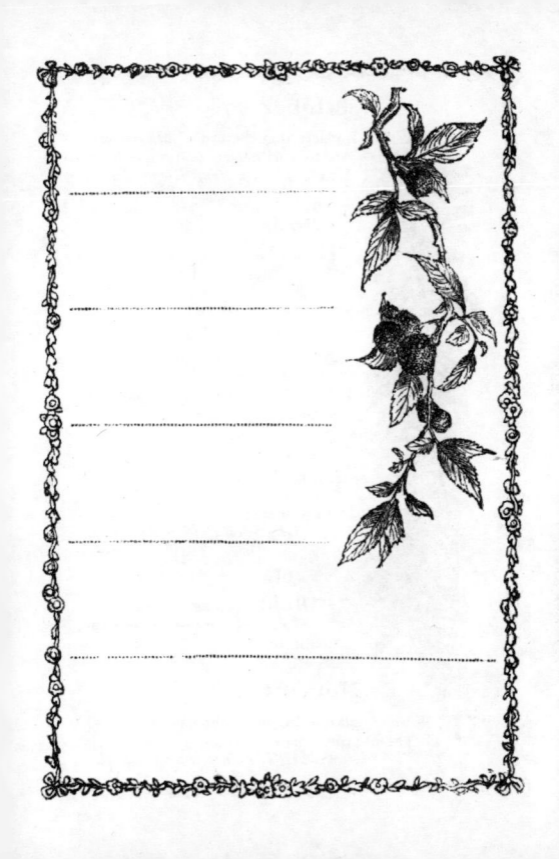

October 27.

ALL places that the eye of heaven visits
Are to a wise man ports and happy
havens. *King Richard II.*

28.

THERE is no music like the voice
Of those we love.
Two Gentlemen of Verona.

29.

SHALL I compare thee to a
summer's day?
Thou art more lovely and more temperate. *Sonnet.*

30.

FRANK nature, rather curious than in haste,
Hath well composed thee.
All's Well that Ends Well.

31.

THERE'S no art
To find the mind's construction in the face. *Macbeth.*

November 1.

'TIS good and needful oft to put men to
The use of their own virtues.
All's Well that Ends Well.

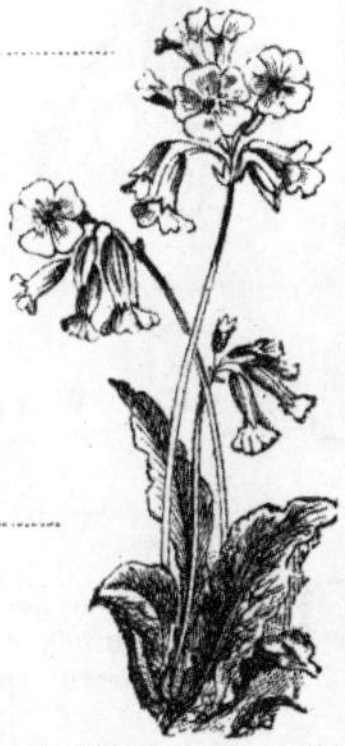

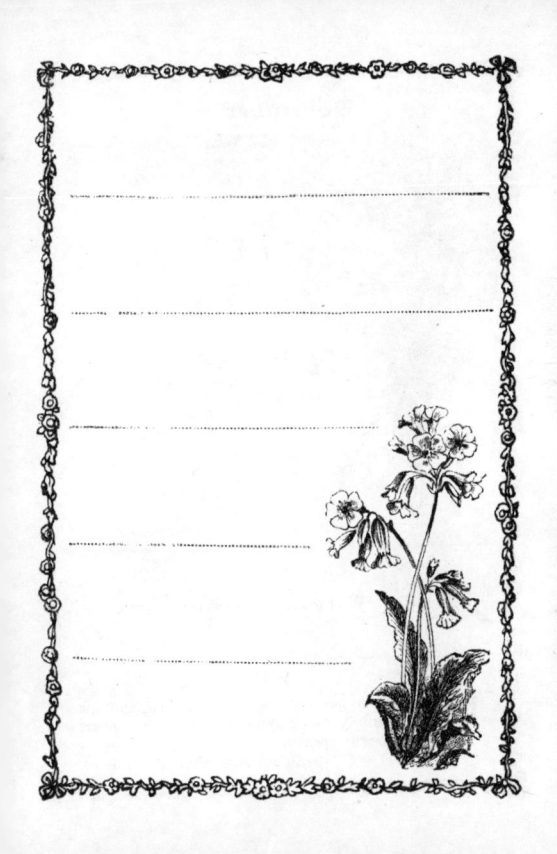

November 2.

SWEET is zealous contemplation.
King Richard III.

3.

A KINDER gentleman treads not the earth.
Merchant of Venice.

4.

THE time of life is short! To spend that shortness basely were too long.
King Henry IV.

5.

IF angels fight, Weak men must fall, for heaven still guards the right.
King Richard II.

6

A FELLOW of plain, uncoined constancy.

King Henry V.

7.

HE hath a heart as sound as a bell, and his tongue is the clapper, for what his heart thinks his tongue speaks.
Much Ado about Nothing.

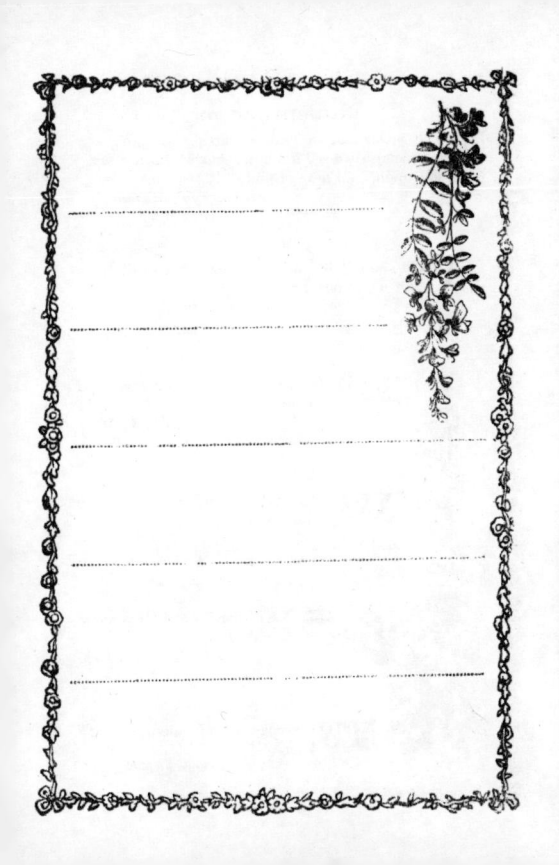

November 8.

THE jewel that we find, we stoop and take't,
  Because we see it; but, what we do not see,
We tread upon, and never think of it.
  Measure for Measure.

9.

AND she is fair, and fairer than that word,
  Of wondrous virtues.
  Merchant of Venice.

10.

LOVE they to live that love and honour have.
  King Richard III.

11.

WINNING would put any man into courage.
  Cymbeline.

12.

SWEETEST nut hath sourest rind.
  As You Like It.

13.

NO revenge is no valour, but to bear.
  Timon of Athens.

November 14.

LET all the ends thou aim'st at be thy country's,
Thy God's, and truth's.
King Henry VIII.

15.

WE must not stint [the fear
Our necessary actions, in
To cope malicious censurers.
King Henry VIII.

16.

HIS own carver and cut out his way,
To find out right with wrong.
King Richard II.

17.

OUR very eyes are sometimes like our judgments—blind.
Cymbeline.

18.

'TIS but a base ignoble mind
That mounts no higher than
a bird can soar.
King Henry VI.

19.

THE hand that hath made you fair hath made you good.

Measure for Measure.

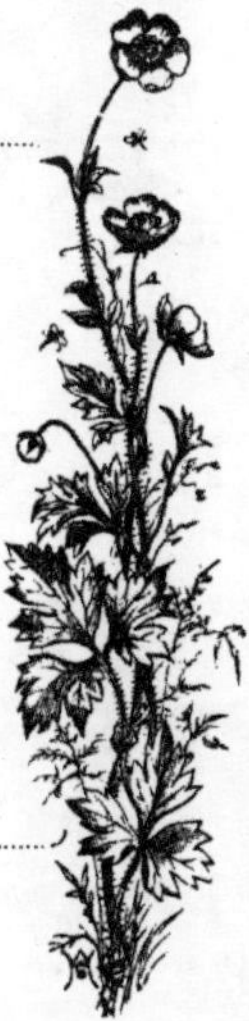

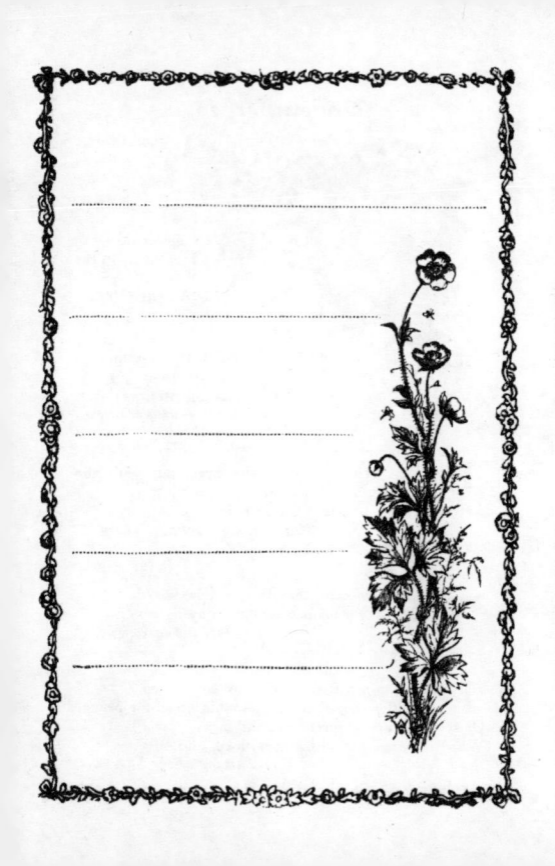

November 20.

A good heart.

K. Hen. V.

21.

IT IS better does not breathe upon the earth.

King Richard III.

22.

FRIENDSHIP is constant in all other things,
Save in the office and affairs of love.

Much Ado about Nothing.

23.

LOVE looks not with the eyes, but with the mind;
And therefore is wing'd Cupid painted blind.

A Midsummer Night's Dream.

24.

SHE is a woman, therefore may be woo'd;
She is a woman, therefore may be won.

Titus Andronicus.

25.

I AM ashamed that women are so simple
To offer war where they should kneel for peace,
Or seek for rule, supremacy, and sway,
When they are bound to serve, love, and obey.

Taming of the Shrew.

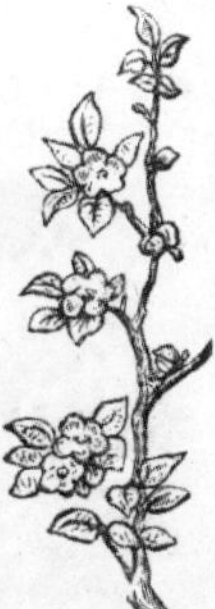

November 26.

HOW would you be,
 If He, which is the top of judgment, should
But judge you as you are?
Measure for Measure.

27.

I AM amazed, methinks, and lose my way
 Among the thorns and dangers of this world.
King John.

28.

OUR wills and fates do so contrary run
 That our devices still are overthrown;
Our thoughts are ours, their ends none of our own.
Hamlet.

29.

MODEST doubt is called
 The beacon of the wise.
Troilus and Cressida.

30.

THIS world to me is like a lasting storm.
Pericles.

December 1

TIME pleases some, tries all.
The Winter's Tale.

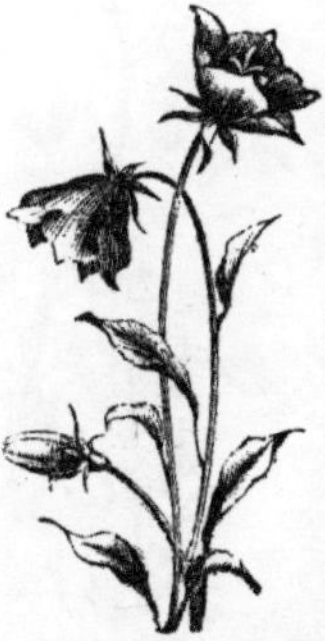

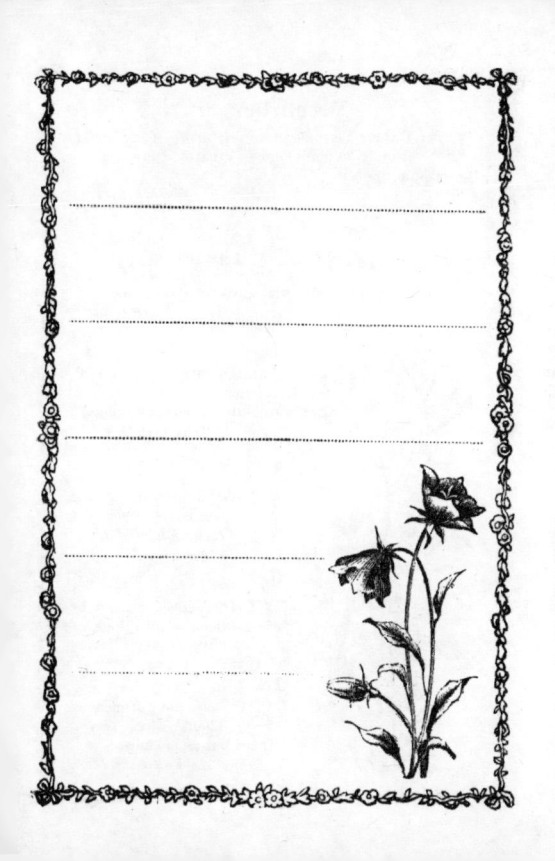

December 2.

LET there be some more test made of my metal,
    Before so noble and so great a figure
Be stamp'd upon it.
Measure for Measure.

3.

GROW great by your example and put on
The dauntless spirit of resolution.
King John.

4.

NOT fearing death, nor shrinking for distress;
But always resolute in most extremes.
King Henry VI.

5.

FIGHT with gentle words.
King Richard II.

6.

THE will of heaven be done in all things.
King Henry VIII.

7.

TO some kind of men
    Their graces serve them but as enemies.
As You Like It.

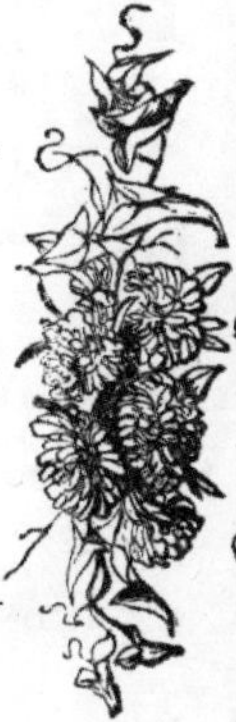

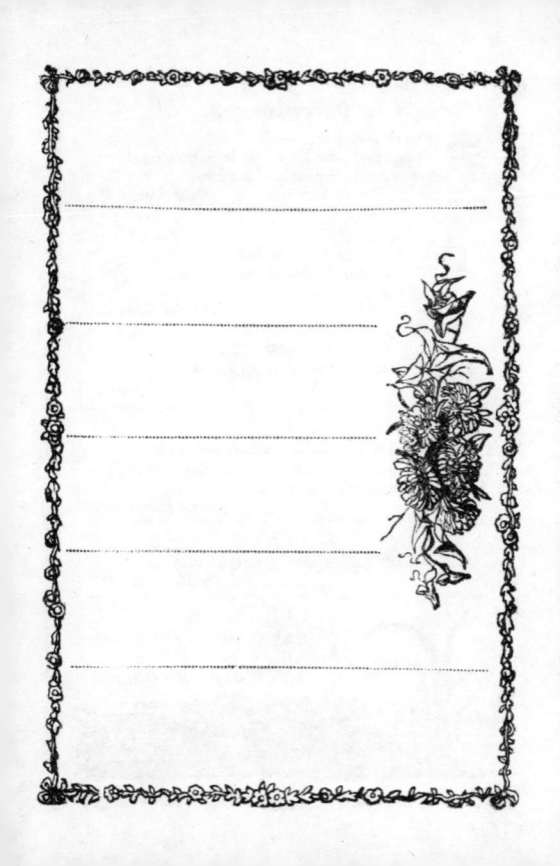

December 8.

SO work the honey-bees,
  Creatures that by a rule in nature teach
The act of order to a peopled kingdom.
King Henry V.

9.

THEN is there mirth in heaven,
  When earthly things made even,
Atone together.
As You Like It.

10.

HIS nature is too noble for the world.
Coriolanus.

11.

IF we do now make our atonement well,
  Our peace will, like a broken limb united,
Grow stronger for the breaking.
King Henry IV.

12.

KINDNESS, nobler ever than revenge.
As You Like It.

13.

I HAVE forgiven and forgotten all.
All's Well that Ends Well.

December 14.

I HOLD it cowardice
  To rest mistrustful where a noble heart
Hath pawned an open hand in sign of love.
King Henry VI.

15.

WE may outrun, at,
  By violent swiftness, that which we run
And lose by over-running.
King Henry VIII.

16.

TO the sessions of sweet silent thought
  Summon up remembrance of things past.
Sonnet.

17.

THE ripest fruit first falls.

King Richard II.

18.

TO the brightest beams distracted clouds give way.
All's Well that Ends Well.

19.

THE best wishes that can be forged in your thoughts be servants to you.
All's Well that Ends Well.

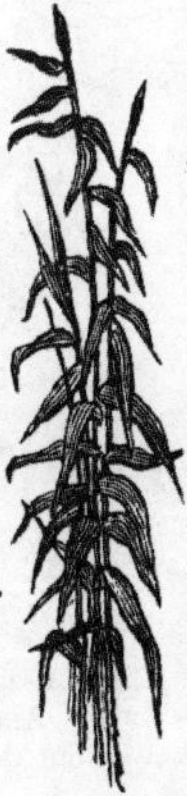

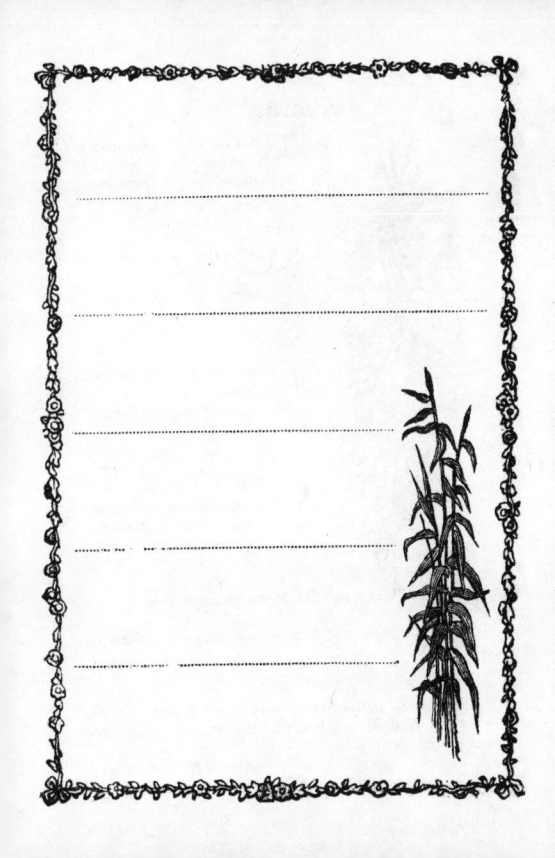

December 20.

THAT season comes wherein our Saviour's birth is celebrated. *Hamlet.*

21.

WHEN good will is showed.
Antony and Cleopatra.

22.

IT is music to hear good deeds.
The Winter's Tale.

23.

GIVE to a gracious message an host of tongues.
Antony and Cleopatra.

24.

NIGHT is now with hymn or carol blest.

A Midsummer Night's Dream.

25.

ALL souls that were, were forfeit once; [took, And He that might the 'vantage best have Found out the remedy.

Measure for Measure.

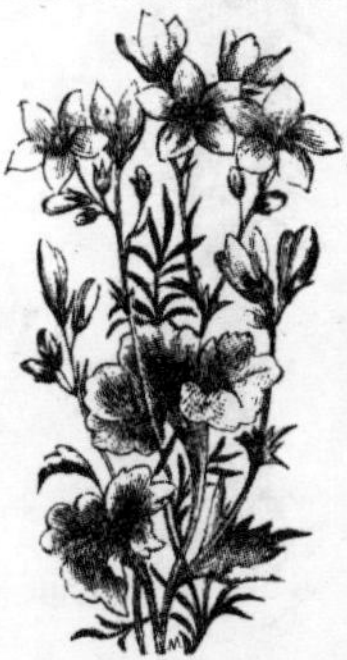

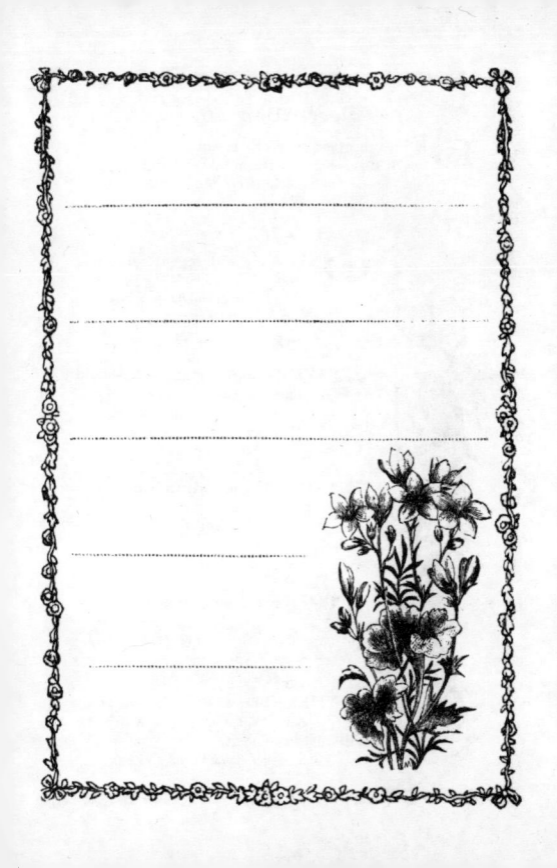

December 26.

HE that of greatest works is finisher
Oft does them by the weakest minister.
All's Well that Ends Well.

27.

ONE never did repent for doing good.
Merchant of Venice.

28.

SAYING and doing well should yoke together.

29.

TAKE all the swift advantage of the hours.
King Richard III.

30.

WE are Time's subjects.
King Henry IV.

31.

THE end crowns all,   [tor, Time,
And that old common arbitra-
Will one day end it.
Troilus and Cressida.

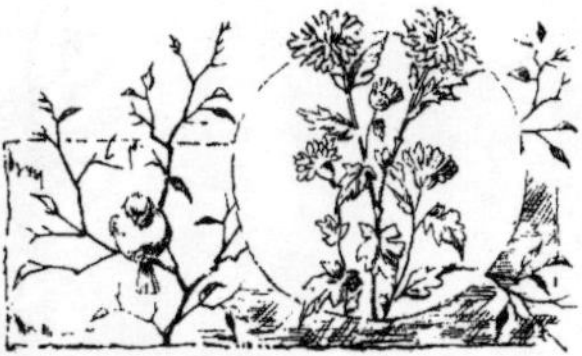

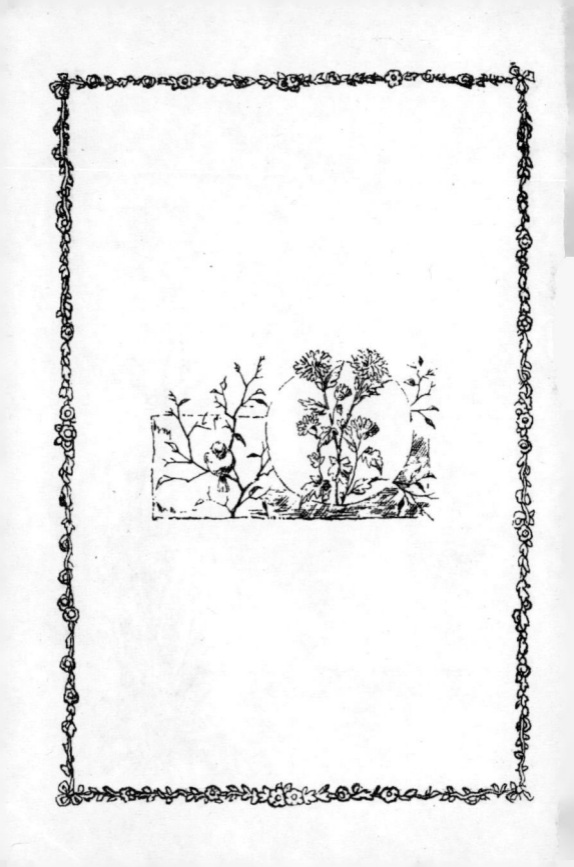

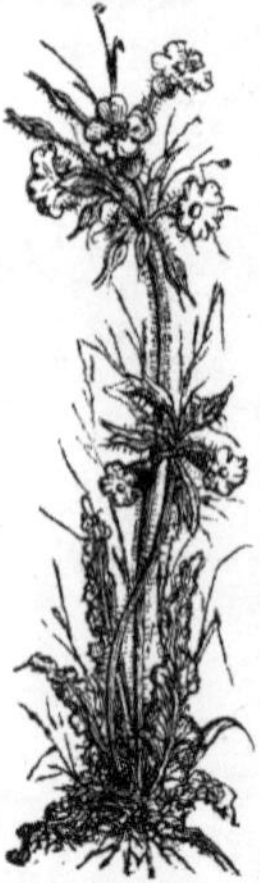

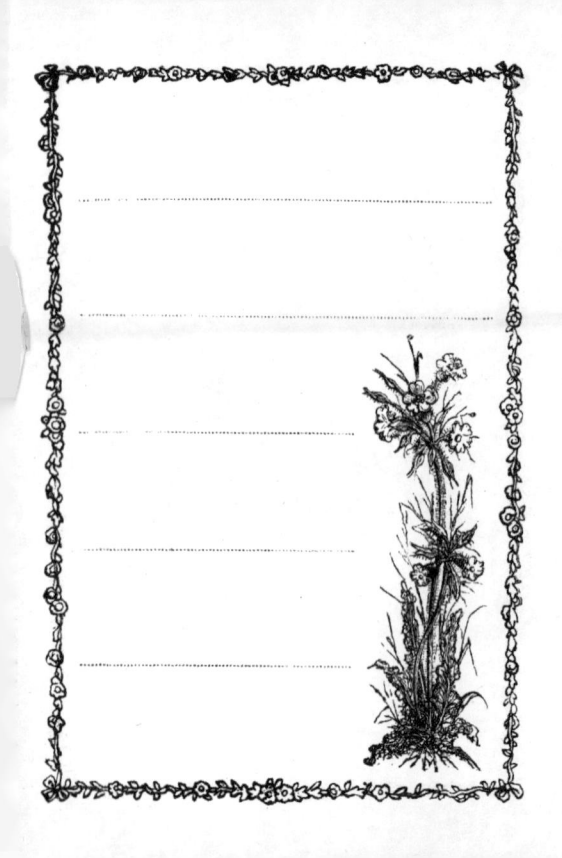